GOOD MORNING

SAM

A story about four remarkable swans

Phyllis M. Washburn

with photographs by

Ralph Washburn

*Enjoy our journey with
Sam and friends.*

Phyllis and Ralph

FIRST EDITION / Softcover
Cover, book design and layout by Ralph Washburn
Edited by Susan E. Smith

ISBN 978-0-9835427-3-5
Printed in The United States of America by
Hanson Printing Company, Brockton, MA 02303-1990

10 9 8 7 6 5 4 3 2 1

Acknowledgments

No book is written without the support of special people. I am indebted to Marion Vuilleumier, mentor par excellence, for her guidance and encouragement to write the story of our adventures with the swans. To my Wordsmyths friends, I am deeply grateful for the friendships of our writers' critique group.

To my husband Ralph mere words can not convey my appreciation for his unfailing support in the writing of this book. Ralph's beautiful swan photography enriches and completes Good Morning Sam.

Introduction

Marion, Massachusetts

My husband Ralph and I had no idea as to the extent of the changes to come into our lives when we first saw the wild mute swan with a broken wing known locally as Sam. What started as a casual act of tossing bread from the wharf to Sam once in awhile evolved into a deep and lasting relationship with this unique swan. In the beginning, our visits were by chance only; then they became daily and within a few month's time the visits were twice a day. This book is an accurate account of our twenty-four year adventures with mute swans.

The mute swan (*Cygnus Olor*) is a large waterfowl of extreme behavior contrasts. The bird is a picture of majestic serenity when at peace with the world, but when provoked the swan is an aggressive and formidable foe. When threatened a swan raises its wings and hisses. Each hiss is louder as the wings rise higher. If this action fails to deter the enemy, the menacing swan charges and strikes the intruder with the bony leading edge of its flailing wings and nips with a sharp bill. To have an agitated swan advancing toward you as it thrashes the air with an eight-foot wing span encourages one to quickly retreat. Thus, we strenuously warn our readers to never approach a wild swan as you would a family pet.

As the relationship grew, so did our knowledge of swans in general and Sam in particular. We became aware of Sam's individual characteristics that defined his personality and made him different from others of his species. Through our experiences with Sam, we had the opportunity to develop unique relationships with three other wild swans as well. Samantha, Little One and Missy, the other swans we knew intimately, also displayed individual characteristics uniquely their own.

Soon, we planned our daily activities with Sam's eating schedule in mind. We looked upon the time spent with Sam as a relaxing interlude in our busy lives.

Sam, because of the missing outer third of his left wing, could not fly and lived in Sippican Harbor year round. He adapted to the winters' severe cold temperatures, the icing of the harbor and the lean food supplies. Howling winter storms found him up on the ice with his head tucked snugly under his wing. During the tropical storms of summer Sam took shelter in a safe inlet protected from the surging tides and strong winds. It amazed us how he wisely chose where to stay during storms. He seemed to be able to predict from which quadrant of the compass the storm winds would blow and chose the safest inlet to stay in while the storm passed by.

Although we had faith in his ability to take care of himself, the threat of a hurricane caused us concern for his safety. In 1985 when Hurricane Gloria started to move up the East Coast of the United States, we decided to take drastic action. We chose to do something that we had never done--capture Sam and confine him for the duration of the storm's fury. Since then, there have been other captures of Sam: once for medical care, twice to rescue him when he was stranded on ice and a few times to place him where we could easily feed him during the winter. At times Sam disagreed with our decisions and did not stay where we put him.

Our adventures with Sam were never dull and routine, always enlightening experiences. Just when we thought we had learned all we could about this wild bird, some new event occurred to prove us wrong. Knowing of the mute swan's aggressive behavior, Ralph and I invariably let Sam decide how quickly our relationship developed. We never forced ourselves into his world but waited for Sam to invite us to be a part of it. What started as a casual happenstance of feeding a mute swan evolved into a twenty-four-year joyous gift of acceptance by these wild birds.

We hope our book will provide entertainment and increase your knowledge of mute swans as you share the joy and wonder of our adventures with Sam. May this book encourage you to diligently observe the world of nature.

Phyllis M. Washburn   April 16, 2010
Ralph G. Washburn

CONTENTS:

Chapter One

THE HURRICANE

"How do we keep that swan safe during the hurricane?" my husband Ralph asked apprehensively, turning the television off after the late evening weather report. "The storm is still moving northwest, so there's a good chance it will move up the east coast and hit us."

"A swan that can't fly doesn't stand a chance against hurricane force winds and a surging tide," I added as we sat worriedly contemplating the possibility of a hurricane. "We have to devise a plan of action."

"It's been more than twenty years since a hurricane has come anywhere near Marion," Ralph recalled. "But this tropical depression is forming where the big hurricanes begin that move northwest to hit our Atlantic coast."

By mid-September 1985, the tropical depression east of the Leeward Islands had quickly developed into Hurricane Gloria. For several days it was only a short blip on our local weather reports. However, our interest piqued as the hurricane headed toward the southeast coast of the United States. Before long, the name Gloria crept into everyone's conversation. Soon neighbors began hauling their boats out of Sippican Harbor.

"Sam takes care of himself in heavy summer storms," I recalled, remembering how the swan always chose a safe area to ride out a storm. It was as though he could predict the direction from which the storm winds would blow. In heavy southeast summer storms he always stayed in an area protected by a south-facing landmass.

"But he has never had to survive a hurricane," Ralph stressed. "Winds of 100 m.p.h. with gusts to 115 m.p.h. will be more than he can handle."

Although we did not know Sam during the Blizzard of 1978, I still shudder when I think of Sam on ice somewhere in Sippican Harbor as the blizzard howled over him. The threat of a hurricane caused us great concern for Sam's safety.

"If he could fly, he probably would go inland to a pond or lake," I said, having read that wild birds usually fly away from large storms. "Without the use of his wings, Sam doesn't have that option."

"I worry about the possibility of a hurricane tidal surge of five to eight feet carrying him deep into the woods lining the harbor where we'd never find him," Ralph said. "Then there is the danger of a boat breaking loose from a mooring and hitting him before he could swim out of the way, or his being decapitated by wind blown debris."

In the darkened bedroom later that night, we were still pondering the problem.

"It might go out to sea," I said, trying to think positively. I knew that sometimes hurricanes headed for the southern New England coast suddenly changed course and veered to the open north Atlantic.

"I don't look for that to happen," Ralph answered. "The only way to be sure Sam is safe is to put him in a building while the hurricane blows over."

"Do you think Sam will let you pick him up?"

"He won't have a choice. I'll just reach down and grab him," Ralph spoke confidently.

"That may shatter the delicate trust Sam has in us," I worried. The thought of not seeing Sam daily was almost unbearable. "He may never again come close to us."

"That's a risk we have to take," Ralph answered. "It's better to have Sam safe and mad at us than to find him dead on a marsh."

As I thought about it, my confidence grew that we could eventually coax Sam to come to us again even if it took a month or two. With winter approaching and his natural food supplies dwindling, hunger would be an incentive for Sam to trust us again.

"We'll only capture him when we know the hurricane will hit," Ralph broke into my thoughts. "But once we have Sam, where do we put him?"

"We can ask Dr. Tremblay if he would keep him at the animal hospital," I suggested. "I wonder what Sam's reaction will be to the capture and confinement?"

"It looks like we are about to find out," Ralph answered. "We'll call the vet first thing tomorrow. Maybe he'll have a suggestion of how to keep Sam safe."

Silence reigned as we thought about Sam and the hurricane, and waited for sleep to come. Tomorrow promised to be a hectic day.

"I am sure Sam will be all right during the hurricane," Dr. Tremblay told us the next day. "However, if you capture Sam I'll keep him here." He left the final decision to us.

The mid-day hurricane reports became even more ominous. Hurricane Gloria was east of the Bahama Islands still heading northwest towards the Carolinas. There was a strong probability that Gloria could skirt along the east coast and make landfall in our area.

As Sam calmly ate at the afternoon feeding, we seriously studied our options for capturing him. That big white bird had no way of knowing what we were planning.

"The storm is still heading northwest, we'll have to capture Sam," Ralph announced after watching the weather report later that evening. "Unless the hurricane's forward movement speeds up, we can wait until late afternoon tomorrow. We'll have only one chance so we must not fail."

I felt a tightening in the pit of my stomach. I dreaded the capture and what it would do to the trusting relationship we shared with Sam.

"I know it must be done but poor Sam, he will not understand why we are picking him up. In fright, he'll thrash you with his wings," I said remembering the bruised shin I received from one of Sam's wings months earlier, "How do you propose to capture that wild bird?"

"We'll bring a sheet with us and coax him ashore to eat. We may have to wait him out, but eventually he'll come to his dish," Ralph said, in his engineer's problem solving style. "Then while he is eating, I'll slip the sheet over him and pick him up."

"It sounds too easy. Don't you expect Sam to put up a fight?" I questioned.

"Don't worry, he won't come to any physical harm," Ralph reassured me. "He'll just be one irate swan for a while."

Arriving to feed Sam the next morning at the Old Landing, we found people taking heed of the hurricane watch, hauling small boats at the ramp. Sam floated nearby, watching the activity and waiting patiently for us. Although he was hesitant because of the activity at the ramp, we coaxed him ashore to eat.

"We won't feed him too much this morning," Ralph said quietly. "We want to make sure he is hungry enough to come up on shore for his supper. Tonight will be our only chance to capture him. Tomorrow morning will be too late according to all the weather forecasts."

All day long as we made hurricane preparations at home, my thoughts kept returning to Sam's capture. With the decision made, my next worry was we would fail to capture him and Sam would die during the hurricane.

We decided to feed Sam at six-thirty since the vet did not begin evening office hours until seven o'clock.

People, concerned over Gloria's predicted arrival, crowded the Old Landing. Weaving our way through the maze of trailers and people, we searched from the south dock for Sam but did not find him.

"He must be at the boat yard," Ralph said. "Probably there's too much going on here."

At the boat yard, we found people hustling to secure their boats before darkness fell. Sam was there and quickly swam toward shore in the quiet water under the dock. I could see he was eager to eat. In the grayness of the falling darkness, his white feathers reflected the last of the day's light.

Dropping the sheet out of Sam's sight, Ralph filled his dish five feet from the water's edge. Without hesitation, Sam walked up to his dish and ate. It had been a wise decision to under feed the swan that morning. He was so hungry he paid no attention to anything but food.

"Its time to pick him up," Ralph said nervously. "Keep him interested in eating."

Moving slowly, Ralph picked up the sheet and quickly dropped it over the eating swan. From under the sheet came a loud protesting honk but no violent thrashing. A split-second later, Ralph picked up the silent bird and carried him to the open station wagon.

I climbed in with the swan while Ralph went back to pick up the food dish. I talked softly to Sam but did not lift the sheet to take a peek. I wasn't at all sure what Sam would do. He might be fighting mad. "You certainly take good care of that swan," called out one woman who often watched us feed and play with him. By this time in our relationship, Sam had attained 'family member' status. Several other people asked Ralph if we were taking Sam home with us.

At the animal hospital, Ralph carried the sheet-covered swan while Dr. Tremblay led the way to Sam's new home. Passing through the wire door, we entered a small 4' x 6' gray cement stall, with just a small window on the outer wall.

Ralph placed the covered swan on the cold slanting floor. Sam's home for the next two days didn't offer much for creature comfort. When Ralph removed the sheet, the vet quickly taped Sam's wings to his body. Sam could easily injure either wing if he flexed them in such a small space, he explained.

Next, I placed his dish in front of him so he could finish his meal. Busy looking about his new surroundings, he ignored the food at first but soon began to eat. Ralph watched from the doorway. After Sam completed his meal, I continued to sit there and play with him.

"He's so calm," I commented. "I had expected a vigorous fight from him."

"He is not threatened by our presence, even in a strange place," Ralph said. "That says a lot about the level of his trust in us. Sam's gift to us is his trusting friendship."

I wondered if it was possible that he knew a storm was coming and we had moved him here for safety's sake. Who can say for sure what goes on inside a swan's mind?

"Good-bye, Sam," I said sadly when it was time for us to leave, "see you tomorrow morning." I wondered if he felt abandoned as he watched us go.

"Do you mind us coming to feed Sam in the morning?" I asked Dr. Tremblay on our way out.

"I plan to be here at eight tomorrow morning," he replied. "I'll feed him if you don't get back here."

"We will be here," Ralph assured the doctor. There was little doubt in our minds that we would feed Sam the next morning. We also wanted to make sure that the swan knew we had not abandoned him.

"Good Morning, Sam," I greeted the swan the following day. He wiggled his tail and gave a head nod in answer. To our surprise, we found him sitting calmly on the floor. We had expected to find a very discontented Sam after he spent the night under a roof.

"He isn't having a hard time adjusting to confinement," Ralph commented as he placed the filled dish in front of the swan. Noisily, Sam gulped down the cornbread as quickly as it fell into his dish.

"I know his wings are taped for a good reason," I said, "but I wish we could remove it." I wondered if he felt a sense of frustration when he tried to flap his wings and couldn't move them.

We brought an extra large ration of food for Sam since we doubted we would be able to feed him that night. Hurricane Gloria was to arrive around noontime and Dr. Tremblay did not plan to return before the next morning. We prolonged our visit with Sam until the doctor was ready to leave. I gave Sam an extra pat and quickly left, happy that he was safe from the hurricane.

The only hint of an approaching storm was the freshening wind and the low dark clouds racing across the light gray sky.

We passed the morning by listening to the hurricane forecasts and wondering how Sam was managing. Although he didn't have any way of knowing, two stalls down from him was a big black dog. If the dog started barking incessantly, would Sam panic and try to escape?

"Shall we go to see Sam?" Ralph suggested at eleven o'clock.

"No one is there," I reminded him.

"We can look through the window," Ralph replied.

As we peeked in the window, a calm, resting swan looked back at us. Was it the sound of our voices or was it visual contact that identified us to him?

"Sam," Ralph called. "How are you doing?" Sam cocked his head for a better look but he did not get to his feet.

"Let's go. I don't want him to think we have food for him," I urged Ralph.

"He shouldn't be hungry after all he ate this morning," Ralph reassured me. "Good-bye, Sam."

At home we sat and waited for Hurricane Gloria. Thankfully, it veered eastward as it marched up the coast. Our area received a glancing blow from the storm by mid-afternoon. We lost our electricity as the winds reached gale force. After the hurricane passed, we resisted the temptation to make another window check on Sam. He would be getting hungry and seeing us could trigger thoughts of food.

When daylight faded, we lit our kerosene lamp and settled down to a cold supper. How dark the world was outside our windows. Here and there, a candle or kerosene lamp illuminated a neighbor's house. I missed the radio and television that kept me in touch with the world. We listened to the battery-powered radio scanner to learn of local emergencies. Flashlights showed the way to bed that night.

Up early the next morning, Ralph fired up the wood stove to perk the coffee and toast the cornbread for breakfast. We arrived at the animal hospital at eight o'clock. The vet opened the door for us.

"Good morning, Sam," I called out walking down the hall. The swan got to his feet as Dr. Tremblay opened the door. Sam wasn't flustered when the doctor used the hose to rinse the slanting stall floor. Although Sam's feathers were dirty and soiled, he had suffered from no other hardship. We decided to feed Sam before returning him to the harbor.

As soon as Dr. Tremblay removed the tape from the swan's wings, Ralph quickly covered Sam with the sheet and carried him to the car. I wondered how Sam felt having the sheet over him again. Half way to the Old Landing, the sheet slipped off Sam's head.

"Well, Sam, what do you think of the view?" I asked as he calmly sat there and looked out the window as we traveled down the road. The driver in the car following us smiled at seeing a swan riding in a car.

People, cars, and trucks clogged the Old Landing. Sightseers with their cameras vied with one another for the best possible spot to record the hurricane damage. Across the water, large sailboats grotesquely littered the now tranquil marsh, each keeled over, as though waiting to sunbathe under a bright September sun.

Weaving through the milling crowd, Ralph backed the car up to the boat ramp. It was then that Sam saw the water for the first time. He vigorously tapped the rear window with his bill. Quickly, I re-wrapped the sheet tightly around his body to prevent him from flapping his wings while Ralph opened the tailgate.

As Ralph carried him down the beach, Sam's feet escaped from the sheet and paddled furiously through the air. Sam's neck, stretched to its fullest extent, pointed directly at the water. Was he reacting to the sensation of flying as Ralph carried him in his arms? In flight, I knew a swan's neck stretches straightforward. The closer to the water he got, the faster his feet moved.

At the water's edge, Ralph placed the swan on the sand and removed the sheet. Without a backward glance, Sam walked into the water and swam directly away from shore. His head repeatedly turned from side to side, but he never did look back.

"The deed is done," Ralph said solemnly. "By nightfall we will know what Sam thinks about his capture."

"He's heading to the cove," I said when he swam toward Black Point. As he disappeared around the rocks, Sam's head was still turning about, surveying his harbor. He seemed to want to get as far away from us and the crowded Old Landing area as possible.

"What did it feel like to carry Sam?" I asked Ralph as we walked back to the car.

"He is an armful of bird! There wasn't much time to think. I was afraid he would try to get out of my arms, I'd lose my hold on him and be thrashed with his wings as he made his escape."

Going home, I felt a strong sense of loss. Would Sam come to eat that afternoon? Was this the end of our friendship with this special swan friend? I thought back to the summer of 1983, when it all began.

*The driver in the car following us smiled at
seeing a swan riding in a car.*

Photo Courtesy M. Mitchell

As Ralph carried him down the beach, Sam's feet escaped from the sheet and paddled furiously through the air. Sam's neck, stretched to its fullest extent, pointed directly at the water.

Chapter Two

FIRST MEETINGS

Ralph was the first to meet Sam. In the early dawn of a midsummer morning of 1983, he arrived at the Old Landing to board a boat for a cruise on Buzzards Bay. In the faint daylight, Ralph saw a large white swan floating alongside the boat.

"Good morning, Sam," skipper MacDougall greeted the swan. "He can't fly because of a broken wing, Ralph. Samson has lived for many years in Sippican Harbor. During boating season, Sam visits the occupied boats looking for food. He especially loves tiny goldfish-shaped crackers, so I always keep some on hand for when he pays us a visit."

"You've got to see this swan," Ralph said to me upon his return home. "This morning he swam right up to the side of the boat to eat the crackers we tossed to him. Let's go to the Old Landing to see if he is there. Bring some bread just in case we find him."

Unfortunately, the swan was not at the Old Landing. However, I met Sam the next day. The beauty and immense size of the mute swan astonished me too. Sam was almost three times larger than a Canada goose with a weight of about thirty pounds. As I watched Sam swim effortlessly while raising his wings slightly in a graceful swan pose, I wondered how a bird as large as he could ever do anything in such a graceful manner.

"Isn't he a beautiful bird?" Ralph asked. "Throw some bread to him. Maybe he'll swim closer to the wharf."

Sitting on the edge of the wharf, I tossed the bread out on the water. Slowly Sam swam towards it, looking carefully at the floating food. Recognizing the bread, Sam ate it and looked for more. This time I tossed the bread a little closer to the wharf. Sam swam to the bread and quickly ate it.

Looking down on the swan, I noticed his large black webbed feet. Everything about the bird was big. His snow white feathers glowed brilliantly against the blue-green water. To me, the swan was a perfect illustration of beauty.

I watched intently as the swan continued to eat the bread. Tossing the last of the bread to Sam, I wished I had more. We watched as Sam swam gracefully away. How beautiful! What a delightful experience it was to scrutinize the mute swan at close range.

The pattern began. From that day on, whenever we went for a walk or a ride, we brought a few slices of bread just in case we saw Sam. Our visits were unscheduled and relatively brief. Sam swam to the wharf, ate the tossed bread, and quickly swam away. As the weeks passed, on occasion Sam seemed to be waiting for us when we arrived at the Old Landing. When he saw us, he swam in anticipation to the south side of the wharf, and patiently waited for me to toss the bread down.

"Let's try to coax Sam to the beach," Ralph suggested one September day. "We can observe him better by looking straight at him rather than always looking down on him." Sam quickly swam over to the beach when he saw us walking in that direction. However, he would not swim too close. To encourage Sam to come nearer, we tossed the bread closer to shore. Cautiously, Sam swam towards the bread, all the while keeping a watchful eye on us. When we made no movement to frighten him, he came forward and ate the bread.

From that day on, we always fed Sam at the beach. While Sam ate, we stood still. However, if we needed to change positions we always executed our movements in slow motion. Although he sometimes stood in the shallow water, he never came ashore.

By late fall, we were feeding Sam daily and enjoying every minute spent with him. Sometimes when we arrived at the Old Landing, we would find him swimming offshore, feeding on the underwater vegetation or nibbling the algae growing on boat moorings. When Sam saw us, he would swim over to the beach to eat.

At that time in our relationship with Sam, our joy came from the trust he displayed by coming to eat at the water's edge. Unknown to us, it was only the very beginning of the deep, trusting relationship that was to develop.

*What a delightful experience it was to scrutinize
the mute swan at close range.*

Chapter Three

WINTER 1983-84

Throughout the fall, we continued to visit Sam daily. How lonely his life became as the days shortened. Gone was the parade of people who visited the Old Landing to check on their boats or to view the picturesque harbor. Now only a few people came to watch us feed Sam.

"Don't move, don't move!" Ralph whispered urgently. Glancing toward the water, I saw the swan swimming toward shore. Reaching shallow water, Sam stood up. As we watched, our swan friend calmly walked up on shore for the first time.

During this time two things changed in our routine. First, as his trust in us grew, Sam began coming up on the beach to eat tossed bread. Floating on water, he looked big but when we saw him standing on land, we were really impressed by his size. Second, the feeding location changed from the Old Landing to the brook behind Tabor Academy's Daggett House when ice covered the water near the beach. Here fresh water, several degrees warmer than the sea water, flowed directly into the brook from an underground stream. Ice covered the brook only when the temperatures fell near zero. It was Sam who chose this feeding spot; we only followed his lead.

The new year of nineteen hundred and eighty-four began with an early morning bike ride to feed Sam. We found him lying out on the ice about fifty feet from shore. Only a small area of the brook had open water for Sam. However, it was enough to satisfy his needs for drinking, bathing and exercising—Sam's basic requirements to make life bearable.

"Sam" Ralph called, "Time to eat."

The swan, still lying down, slowly began to move. Using his large feet much like a cross-country skier used ski poles; Sam pushed his resting body over the ice. It took him several minutes to complete this task as his webbed feet had little traction and often lost contact with the slick surface.

"You can do it, Sam" I encouraged the struggling swan.

How I wished we could help him. Alas, this was one of those life experiences that we were powerless to alter. Sam had to do this for himself. Much to our relief, Sam was soon swimming towards shore and the waiting food.

During the summer, Sam had taken care of his essential food requirements. As winter settled in and the growth of sea grasses and algae halted, Sam depended on people to subsidize his meager food supply. Watching him devour the bread, I doubted that Sam had anyone else feeding him now. In a matter of minutes, the breakfast was over and the swan returned to the water.

Because of his paddle shaped feet, Sam was an excellent swimmer and once in the water he was in complete control of all situations. He was a formidable opponent in any challenging conflict with an adversary. Sam's feet extended fully as he used them, one at a time, to push himself through the water. Then each webbed foot folded like an accordion pleated hand fan as he brought it forward to start another pushing stroke. How astonishingly those feet, without any wasted motion, worked for Sam. On land, he was at a disadvantage. His walking was slow; he lumbered and waddled up the uneven shore no longer the picture of graceful movement. He looked like a large cumbersome duck!

When we returned to Sam's winter home later that afternoon, he was swimming in the small patch of open water. Against the monochromatic grays of the scenery, Sam's feathers seemed to radiate a vivid white glow of their own. Everything looked and felt as cold as the east wind that penetrated our winter clothing. The constantly blowing wind rustled through the crisp, brown leaves that hung tenaciously to the scrub oaks lining the marshy inlet. The low gray clouds dropped a heavy shower of snow flurries that swirled about us and then quickly ceased.

One look at the dismal scene made me glad I was not a swan. Other than Sam, there wasn't one inviting feature in the whole area. For Sam, it was the best of poor choices of winter homes. Sam stood in the shallow water, stretched his wings, settled back down, and swam to shore. He was handsome, even with the broken wing that kept him in Sippican Harbor year round. Without that handicap, I knew that Sam, like others of his species, would have flown farther south for the winter. Mute swans generally do not migrate great distances. They spend the severe winters on the open waters of the Atlantic Coast from Rhode Island to the Carolinas. Some swans, when inland lakes and ponds freeze, only migrate to the Southern New England coastal waters.

Reaching the water's edge, Sam walked ashore as he had done so often before. This time as he came up to me, Sam grabbed my pant leg with his bill and softly "grunted" while he held on. Sam was talking to me, in his way. He gave no sign of being angry or feeling threatened since he held his wings close to his body. I knew that when swans sense danger, the first visual sign is the raising of their wings over their backs. The greater the peril, the higher the wings rose.

"Good morning, Sam," I spoke softly. "Are you hungry?"

As Sam continued to hold onto my pant leg, I dared to do something I had never done before. I ever so slowly reached down and gently touched the soft, cool feathers on Sam's back at the base of his neck. He "honked" at me but did not become alarmed by my touch.

What a wonderful sensation! The feathers felt very soft but there was an inner firmness to them. I did not repeat the touch, fearing Sam would return to the water without eating. The night promised to be cold and Sam would need his food as fortification against the falling temperatures.

When Sam looked for his food, I opened the bread bag and started to feed the now impatient swan. Quickly, Sam ate all the bread I had and waddled back to the water.

Ralph usually stayed in the car while I fed Sam. He didn't want to scare the swan and have him return to the water before he completed his meal. As we left, Sam began swimming in the classic swan position: head high, a graceful curve to his long slender neck, with the body held in a majestic stance. His swimming posture gave us every indication he was content with life at that moment.

The next morning we found Sam out on the ice behind Daggett House with his feet tucked neatly into his side feathers and his head tucked safely under a wing. It would have been easy to mistake Sam for an ice-covered rock. There were no particular features to suggest the

mound was a swan: no black feet protruding from under the mass of frost-covered feathers, no long neck extended fully as he surveyed his domain. To our amazement, we realized Sam was sleeping!

A few seconds later, when a sound piqued his attention, Sam raised his head. Noticing my presence, he slowly pushed himself to where the thin ice gave way under his weight. Once in the water, Sam swam through the paper-thin ice, creating a gentle ripple in its soft surface. Every so often Sam placed his bill in the mushy surface. At first I thought he was drinking, but closer observation revealed Sam was probably testing the thickness of the ice. The soft ice crumbled easily under the pressure of his bill, creating a trim of icy slush around his body. Upon reaching the open patch of water, Sam quickly assumed the regal swan pose. How stately Sam looked as he swam toward his waiting breakfast.

This time I offered Sam something new—corn flakes. "Well that wasn't such a bright idea, Sam," I said as he ate some while the rest quickly sank to the bottom of the inlet. "They don't float long enough for you to eat them." Obviously, corn flakes were not ideal swan food.

Soon we had unwelcome guests; gulls flew overhead. When the harbor froze, the gulls gathered wherever we fed Sam. First one gull, then two, then another and before long a large flock of gulls was circling noisily over head. They descended to the water some distance from shore and patiently waited to grab any food Sam might miss. I did not encourage the gulls for they could be noisy, quarrelsome nuisances. In a few minutes, as predicted, the gulls were aggressively fighting over some bread that had floated beyond Sam's reach. Because of the noisy gulls, Sam ate quickly and left, refusing to come ashore that morning. The combative activity of the gulls must have made him feel uneasy. I noted Sam only came ashore when he knew it was completely safe for him.

A couple of mornings later, we found Sam some distance from shore, sitting on solid ice. Alternating pockets of ice and open water lay between Sam and us. "Good Morning, Sam," I called to him. He turned his head in answer to my call. Sam stood up and waddled to the edge of the first batch of open water, sat on the ice and with his feet pushed himself into the water. Quickly, he swam to the second patch of solid ice. He stopped, swam to the right along the ice edge looking for an opening to swim through, but not finding one he started to swim in the opposite direction. He swam the whole length of the ice before he realized he was swimming away from us. Sam turned about and swam back, still searching for an open passage through the impeding ice. He repeated the whole process again before becoming convinced there was no opening in the solid ice mass. He swam back toward the spot where he was directly across from us and then slowly climbed onto the ice.

This was the first time we witnessed Sam getting up on ice. By thrashing his feet in the water, he raised his body slightly, propelled himself forward, grabbed the ice edge with one foot and landed the front third of his body on the ice edge. Then using his other foot, he got half of his body up on the ice. Using first one foot then the other, he slowly pushed himself away from the ice edge. He seemed to know when he had pushed himself far enough, for he stood up on his feet, stretched his wings and tried to walk. He made slow progress over the slick ice, slipping and sliding many times. When he finally reached the ice edge closest to us, he again sat down and pushed himself into the open water. We applauded as Sam conquered his obstacles. In a minute or two, the swan was standing in front of me, waiting for his food. Impatiently he nipped at my pant leg to gain my attention.

"Okay, Sam, I'm getting your food as fast as I can. It was clever how you got yourself over the ice. You're a smart, old bird!" I felt a harsh pinch on my leg. "Sam, you should not bite the hand that feeds you," I scolded my swan friend. Even a small nip was painful because of the sharp front edge of his upper bill. The swan's upper bill protruded over a serrated lower bill. The lower bill is used to pull the grasses while the upper bill cuts them.

Sam ate quickly and returned to the water. When he hissed softly, I turned to see what prompted this. A dog had silently come up behind me. Sam somehow knew the dog was not a threat to him because the hiss that he gave was more of a warning signal than a battle cry. Not threatened by the swan's gentle hiss; the dog turned and calmly walked away. Sam slowly paddled away from shore to begin his morning bath.

When I returned for the afternoon feeding, I found the open water almost empty. A small gathering of mallard ducks huddled together where the stream entered the inlet. Each duck had its feathers fluffed up against the deepening cold. Although they saw me, they did not take to the air, reluctant to relinquish the meager warmth of their resting place.

In the gathering darkness, I faintly saw Sam out on the ice thirty feet from shore, all settled down for the night with his head tucked under his wing. I was too late to feed Sam his supper. Then I realized for the first time it was the daylight and darkness that Sam lived by, not the ticking of a clock. If the day had been sunny, Sam would have still been swimming about. I decided I must come earlier on dark and dreary days.

The next morning Ralph and I drove out on the Old Landing wharf to see where Sam was before going to the inlet. Our swan friend was awake and swimming about his winter home. He saw us and when I arrived at the inlet, he was already on shore, waddling towards me as I walked down the embankment with the bread bag in hand.

"Sam, I'm sorry that I did not get here on time yesterday afternoon. Breakfast will taste extra good this cold morning." He responded by tugging at my sleeve, next he grabbed on to my pant leg.

With Sam so close, I decided to touch him again. As he held my pant leg in his bill, I slowly stroked the underside of his long graceful neck. He showed no signs of concern. My movements were gentle and slow. How marvelous it felt to be stroking a wild bird and to have him consent to my touches. His feathers, covered by tiny ice droplets, felt cool to my hand.

The one-to-one touching did not last more than a minute or two and then Sam was actively looking for his food. I retrieved the dropped bread bag and served Sam breakfast. The joy of that morning's experience lingered with me throughout the day.

During the January thaw, Sam was able to swim south to Tabor's dock, where we fed him. As the ice melted along the shore, Sam roamed the whole distance of open water. At mealtimes we would find him either behind Daggett House or within sight of the dock.

With the return of cold weather in early February, Sam was again icebound and he seemed glad to have our food. There were days when Sam would not come ashore for some reason known only to him. Whenever he did, I touched him gently as he held onto my sleeve or pant leg. To my amazement, it never alarmed him. Ralph enjoyed witnessing the trusting bond building between Sam and me. We did everything in our power not to shatter the delicate relationship between this wild bird and ourselves. By early March the ice line receded as the stronger sunshine warmed the water. Sam swam farther and farther away from his winter home as more of the harbor opened up. Usually he was around at mealtimes, but not always. When he did not show up for a meal, we felt sure it was because he was able to satisfy his food needs for that day. There had to be some natural food in the areas previously covered by the winter's ice.

We, too, were glad to feel the warmth of the March sun on our hands and faces, although the gusty winds at our backs still had a cold bite. We no longer needed to worry about how Sam was doing during snowstorms and deep freezes.

A small gathering of mallard ducks huddled together where the stream entered the inlet

Chapter Four

SPRING AND SUMMER SURPRISES

After months of being ice bound in one area, Sam seemed to enjoy his newly returned freedom. It appeared that freedom was a treasured condition, even for a swan. Sam went on long swimming sojourns, conducting close inspection of his favorite areas of the harbor. Although the March winds made us shiver, Sam appeared pleased with the arrival of the cold spring days. With the change of seasons, Ralph and I discovered new aspects of his behavior. By this time, Ralph joined me at the beginning of each feeding session with Sam

In early April, we had our first opportunity to witness Sam's reaction to geese. One morning we arrived at the Old Landing to find four Canada Geese swimming with Sam. As we fed Sam at the water's edge the geese slowly swam toward shore looking for food. In warning, Sam raised his wings as the geese came nearer.

"Don't worry, Sam," I spoke gently. "There is plenty of food to go around."

The geese kept swimming forward. The swan raised his wings even higher and turned towards the approaching geese with his neck long and head low. Wisely, the geese heeded Sam's warning stance and moved to the farther side of the boat ramp.

As Sam completed his breakfast, Ralph tossed bread to the geese. For a while, swan and geese concentrated on satisfying their hunger. Before long Sam became aware that Ralph was feeding the geese. He showed his displeasure by walking back into the water with his wings up and his head held low. I knew that among waterfowl this posture conveys aggression. He apparently did not intend to share his food.

"Sam, come back!" I commanded. He quickly displayed his full battle posture—wings high, long neck curled up and forward in a loop with head held down in a menacing position—as he charged towards the geese. Obviously, the geese understood the threat because they forgot all about eating and hastily retreated from the advancing swan.

When Sam closed in on them, the geese separated—one pair swam northward while the other pair headed south. Now Sam had to choose which pair to chase. He swam northward.

"Look what's happening" Ralph observed.

While Sam chased the first pair, the second pair was swimming back towards us and the waiting food. As Sam caught up to the fleeing geese, the male separated from the female, honking loudly as he swam southeastward. Sam chose to swim after the noisy male goose, gaining speed as he went. Just when he was within reach, the goose took to the air, flying a short distance away. Sam gave up the chase, lowered his wings and turned to swim back to the shore. Then Sam saw the second pair of geese eating our tossed bread. Up went the wings as he charged towards the feeding geese. Seeing the hostile swan, the geese swam in a wide arc around him and headed southward. Sam altered his course accordingly and continued the chase.

"Look," Ralph said, "the first pair is coming together again."

I looked in the direction he was pointing and saw the geese greet one another with head dipping and loud honking that got Sam's attention. Again he changed his course and swam towards the incoming geese.

"It's a circus. Now the second pair is swimming toward shore as Sam chases the others," Ralph continued. "Sam is being outsmarted."

This pair made it to shore. As they devoured the bread, I admired their beauty. Their back feathers looked like a rich tapestry with each brown feather tip delicately etched with a tawny line. Their head and neck feathers shimmered like black satin. A white band circuited under their chins trimming each cheek with a triangular patch, and their eyes looked like smooth, jet-black glass beads. The soft, delicate pink of the inner mouth was in sharp contrast to the black bill. The dusty gray-brown of the chest and underbelly gave way to vivid white feathers on the rear underside that contrasted with the black tail feathers. Their feet were as black as their bills. Though I longed to touch them, I realized any attempt to do so would end the joy of having them so close to me. I imagined their feathers would feel much like Sam's—cool, soft but firm to the touch. Their voices gave a soft musical honking as they seemed to plead, "More bread, please."

After a while, Sam stopped chasing the retreating geese, his wings came down and he swam towards shore. Sam had totally lost interest in the chase. He stood in the shallow water and began preening his feathers. The feeding geese, no longer intimidated by Sam's now docile posture, continued to eat. Momentarily the other geese joined the pair on the beach, noisily honking their greetings. Soon harmony prevailed: four geese sharing bread and one swan busily preening.

The next morning, Sam was some distance from the Old Landing but the Canada Geese were waiting for bread. As I sat on my stool, they quickly walked up the beach, coming to a halt a short distance away. As I tossed bread to the geese, one ventured close enough to be hand fed. The gentleness of the goose's bite surprised me. It was nothing like the harsh pinch of Sam's bill.

Soon Sam noticed me feeding the geese and headed for shore. As he plowed through the water at top speed, the water rippled up his chest and along his sleek body, creating a small wake. Reaching the shallow water, he got up on his feet and charged up the beach to me. The geese scattered in all directions.

"Well, Sam, are you hungry or are you jealous about who is eating your bread?" I asked.

Sam ate most of his meal before beginning to evict the geese. The same 'chase the geese' game played yesterday was repeated as geese and swan forgot all about food.

As the days passed, we witnessed this scenario on numerous occasions. Finally, the geese flew away to find nesting sites. Once more, mealtimes were calm and peaceful for Sam.

With the launching of the first boat of the season, we discovered another of Sam's behaviors. At the end of one feeding visit, Sam was back in the water preening when a boat arrived for launching at high tide. Seeing the boat trailer backing down the ramp, the swan stopped his preening. Sam's wings came up in full battle height; he laid his long neck back between the raised wings with his bill resting on the underside of his neck. He charged at the offending boat trailer as it entered the water. When Sam reached the boat, he brought his head up and forward, and attacked the stern of the boat. Then he circled around and charged at the boat again. He repeated the assault until the boat was floating freely in the water. Next, Sam resumed his battle position and swam in charging circles around the boat as the man tried to start the stubborn engine. Finally the motor came to life; sputtering and belching smoke as some cold outboard engines do. The boat moved away from the ramp. Sam chased after the receding boat until it was well out in the harbor.

With more and more boats being launched, we witnessed Sam's reactions many times. If the boat anchored within sight of the Old Landing, Sam followed it all the way to its mooring and continued his harassing tactics for an hour or more. He charged at the boat with his wings raised but when he reached it, the wings came down. He'd nip at its bow or stern and then swim the length of the boat rubbing his body against it.

"Is he trying to repel an enemy or cultivate a friendship?" Ralph asked as we watched Sam nip the latest launched boat.

"It might be he does not want the boats in his harbor and he's protesting in swan fashion," Ralph suggested an answer to his own question. Sam played this game with each newly launched boat until there were a dozen or more boats anchored in the harbor, then this behavior ended. Maybe he sensed he had lost the battle as the number of boats in the harbor increased steadily as warmer weather arrived.

Each following spring Sam defended his territory in this manner. A friend once asked if I could keep Sam away from his boat after it was launched since he feared that Sam's bill would mar the fresh paint.

"I'm afraid I have no control over that swan," I answered. "Only Sam decides what he will do!"

After launching at the Old Landing, the friend solved the problem by tying his boat up at Island wharf, well hidden from Sam. Most days, Sam swam near the Old Landing and seldom ventured southward to Island wharf. My friend's boat remained unmarred by swan bites.

With the arrival of summer, we noticed changes in Sam's feeding habits. As his natural food supply became ample, he did not always come to eat. Often we saw Sam feeding himself. One of his favorite eating areas was the quiet inlet at the head of the harbor. Here Sam had the water to himself, as the inlet held many hidden rocks at high tide and little water at low tide. Some days we walked over the marsh to visit him there.

One cloudy June afternoon we walked down to the inlet to see Sam. We had not fed him for a couple of days and we missed visiting with him. We found him eating sea grasses.

"Sam, Sam," I called. He kept on dipping his head underwater for grass and paid no attention to my calls.

"He hears us. Probably, he's not very hungry," Ralph said. "Each time he brings his head out of the water, he has a long blade of eel grass in his bill. He doesn't really need our food now."

"The bread and crackers we feed him probably don't have much food value for a swan," I remarked. "His natural food is healthier for him."

Patiently, I kept calling and offering a cracker to the swan. After a while Sam swam towards me. Since it was not a normal feeding place, he seemed reluctant to swim too close to shore. Finally, he swam close enough to stretch his long neck to its limit to reach the offered cracker. Ever vigilant, Sam grabbed the cracker and quickly drew back. Again the long neck stretched forward and took another cracker.

"See, Sam. It's safe here. We won't harm you," I spoke softly. However, after eating only a small amount of food, Sam swam away.

As Sam left, two Canada geese families came to eat. Each family swam in a single file, with a parent at each end of the line. The fluffy yellow-brown goslings peeped softly, as they followed along. As the geese approached, Sam swam back with his wings raised. Although Sam was not hungry, it appeared he did not want the geese to eat. He chased both families across the inlet to the farther bank. The geese scampered up the uneven shoreline and flapped their wings in victory as the swan ended the chase. I had read that waterfowl signal victory in a battle with an adversary by vigorously flapping their wings at the end of the encounter.

Sam swam a short distance to the mouth of the small fresh water brook that emptied into the inlet. There he drank the fresh water that floated on the surface of the heavier seawater. Although Sam's body could assimilate salt water, fresh water was the preferred choice.

As Sam began to preen, the geese walked quietly down the embankment and silently slipped into the water. This time the geese reached the large rock I was sitting on and I tossed bread to them as they gathered around me. The goslings looked like loosely wound balls of yellow-brown angora yarn. Their necks were short and their bills matched the brown of their fleecy feathers.

"Their feathers blend into the color of the old grass stubs lining the bank," I marveled. "It is difficult to locate them in the marsh stubble. Only faint peeps give away their hiding place."

"You better get off that rock soon," Ralph suggested.

I looked over my shoulder and saw the rock was fast becoming an island with the incoming tide. It was time to vacate my position or I would have to wade to shore. Tossing the remaining bread to the geese, I jumped to shore.

My movement caught Sam's attention and he saw the geese feeding. Again, he swam over with his wings high.

Each family gathered its offspring in single line formation, with a mother goose at the front and father bringing up the rear, and swam out of the inlet with the swan in pursuit. At first, both families swam

together. Then they separated and each family headed in a different direction. After choosing which family to chase, Sam rapidly closed the distance between them. When he was within reach of the larger male goose, the goose separated from his family and swam away, honking loudly. Of course, Sam swam after the noisy goose while the female stealthily steered the quiet goslings away from the menacing swan and back to the safety of the now flooded bank, concealing them in the tall marsh grass. When Sam and the goose he was chasing reached the farther bank, the goose took to the air and flew back to his family. Sam, seeming to have lost interest in the chase, continued swimming out of the inlet.

A few days later, we found Sam, with his wings down, swimming with a mother duck and her babies. Mother Duck accepted his peaceful presence. It was as if he was the ducklings' visiting uncle.

Now, Sam's feeding visits with us became variable and short. Often, on warm sunny days, we found him up on a bank sleeping soundly. Sometimes we watched as he satisfied his hunger by dipping his head underwater to eat the favored eelgrass or nibbled algae from moorings. Other times we observed him visiting occupied boats begging for food. Sam's carefree wanderlust summer life was in total contrast to his harsh life during the winter months.

Several days later, we found Sam, with his wings down, swimming with a mother duck and her babies. Mother duck accepted his peaceful presence. It was as if he was the ducklings' visiting uncle.

Chapter Five

MIGRATION SAM STYLE

When the 1984 duck hunting season began in late November, we often saw early morning hunters stationed in the marshes lining the harbor waiting for the arrival of unsuspecting waterfowl. Some days we awoke to the sound of shotguns shattering the quiet dawn. Our thoughts always turned quickly to Sam's safety. We were helpless to stop the guns that probably terrified him.

On the morning of December 14 we heard repeated shooting in the area of Hammett Cove. Each volley caused us to hasten to Sam. Arriving at the Old Landing, we saw two hunters positioning themselves behind the large rocks at the southern end of Black Point. A black hunting dog trotted around, his nose busily tracking a scent. Silhouetted against the eastern horizon, a third hunter in a canoe was placing the decoys in the calm water surrounding the point of land. What was there about hunting that induced men to leave warm houses to stand in the cold December air waiting for a chance to end a creature's life?

Silently, we searched the area for Sam. "I don't see him. Do you?" Ralph asked, breaking into my thoughts.

"No. I was so sure that we'd find him in the brook behind Daggett House. I doubt he's in the cove this morning."

"Look with the binoculars," Ralph suggested. "Maybe he's down around Tabor's dock. He may have gone down there to get away from the hunters."

Once hunting season began, the swan kept to the western shore of the inner harbor. Whenever he heard a gun fired, Sam would bring his head straight up, turning it from side to side as if he was searching the area to find the source. There seemed to be a sense of apprehension in his movements. Although the hunters were not shooting at him, Sam had no way of knowing that. To me he appeared to display a fearful demeanor. I searched the dock area hoping to catch a glimpse of our friend.

"Nothing. Let's drive to Tabor and Island wharf; maybe he's in one of the small inlets."

Our search was fruitless. The western shore was empty; there were no hunters on this side of the harbor. We returned to the Old Landing. Off Black Point, the floating decoys bobbed gently in the calm water surrounded by ribbons of mist, providing the familiar scene with a dismal aura that matched our somber mood.

"Where do you suppose he is?" I asked anxiously. We had always located him whenever he roamed away from his usual feeding area. Bang! Bang! Bang! Gunfire shattered the quiet morning. Looking across to Black Point, I saw a wisp of smoke drift upward. Not seeing any geese flying erratically away, I wondered why the hunters had fired their guns.

"We can check Hammett," said Ralph. "It's just possible he spent the night in the cove and will not come out because of the hunters stationed at the entrance of the cove. If he's not there, we'll check Planting Island Cove. He has to be somewhere in the harbor. He can't fly."

We did not find Sam anywhere. Ralph went to work and I returned home. At mid-morning, I again searched Sam's favorite eating places. Still, Sam remained missing. By noontime, our concern for Sam had heightened. This time we searched along both sides of the Converse Point shoreline.

"Where is he?" Ralph anxiously asked. There was no answer to give.

By late afternoon, Sam still had not returned. Again, we searched every place we had earlier in the day. As darkness fell, we despairingly headed home with Sam's uneaten food. While there had been other days when Sam did not come to eat, we usually saw him off in the distance. Maybe the gunfire of the morning had driven him farther out into the open water of the outer harbor.

The next day, Saturday, massive gunfire awakened us. We wasted no time in getting to the Old Landing. Surely, Sam would be hungry this morning. However, Sam was not there to greet us. The thin fog drifted aimlessly in the still morning air like a giant coverlet of the angel hair once used to trim our Christmas tree. In the far distance, we heard the crack of gunshots, echoing off the eastern shore. Again, we searched the shoreline without locating the missing swan.

"It's no use," Ralph gave voice to our darkest thoughts. "We have looked everywhere we can imagine he might go. Something terrible has happened to our friend otherwise he'd come for breakfast."

Sadly, we returned home, each with an empty ache in the center of our being. Our world was incomplete. That was the day each of us realized how attached we had become to that big, white bird.

At mid-morning Ralph telephoned the harbormaster. "Chris, Sam is missing. We haven't seen him since Thursday afternoon. We think he may be the victim of a hunting accident and is hiding in some isolated inlet. We have searched as much of the shoreline as we can by car and on foot. If you are out in your patrol boat today, would you look for Sam?"

Later that afternoon the harbormaster telephoned. "I've searched the harbor; all the way to Silvershell. I even checked Hammett and Planting Island coves but did not find Sam. Don't worry. I'm sure he's all right as there isn't any evidence to prove otherwise."

Next, Ralph called the Police Department. "The injured swan, Sam, is missing. Would you call me if you receive a report of anyone finding an injured swan?"

Our prospects of finding him dimmed with the passage of time. There was nothing else we could do but continue our periodic searches of the harbor. There was the slight chance that somehow the harbormaster had missed seeing Sam. Any hope, no matter how small, was better than no hope at all. Night fell with Sam still missing. Our fears seemed to have come true. Two days had passed without seeing him.

Sunday morning dawned with a solid cloud cover. The harbor was quiet; Sundays were true days of peace for no hunting was allowed. However, Sam was not waiting for us at the Old Landing when we arrived. We mechanically went about our daily chores in between numerous trips to the shore to search for our missing friend. Another day ended dismally.

Then Tuesday, Ralph called me from work saying, "I just got a call from the police." My heart stopped beating for a moment. "They just received a call from a woman in east Marion. She has seen a swan swimming in the Weweantic River near Dexter's wharf," he continued as my heart began its normal rhythm again. "She also said the swan seemed to have an injured wing." Although my hopes soared, I was cautious; it couldn't be our missing Sam! More likely, it was another injured swan. "Drive over to see if it is Sam," Ralph said. "Let me know what you find."

Quickly, I drove to Dexter's wharf, all the while telling myself not to get too hopeful. It didn't seem possible that Sam could swim such a long distance through the rough waters of the outer west entrance to the Cape Cod Canal. It was quite a navigational feat for a non-flying bird. Normally swans flew when changing feeding sites some distance away. Sam did not have that option. Buzzards Bay is turbulent because of the changing tidal currents through the Cape Cod Canal and the prevailing southwest winds. Like other swans, mutes prefer the calmer waters of the coastal inlets to the choppy seas.

My heart flipped when I saw a swan sitting out on a rock, busily preening its feathers. Since it was facing eastward, the swan did not see me. Walking out on the wharf, I called, "Sam, Sam!" Quickly, the head came up and turned towards me. It was Sam! "What are you doing over here?" I asked as my heart fluttered with joy. "Are you lost?" His look at me seems to say, `Where have you been? What took you so long?'

Sam slipped into the water and swam cautiously towards me for this was not the familiar feeding place. When he was within reach, I tossed some bread to him. He ate it and quickly came forward for more food. Suddenly my world was warm and sunny although it was a very cold, cloudy, December morning.

Upon returning home, I telephoned Ralph to share the good news. For him, the wait had been longer. "That little devil!" he exclaimed as the worry of the past five days slipped away and his voice held the same joy that I felt in my heart as we shared the knowledge of Sam's safety. "What possessed him to swim to the Weweantic River?" questioned Ralph. "The river is not very wide; there's a greater chance of him getting hit by a hunter's stray bullet. At least in Sippican Harbor, the local hunters know of Sam's presence. How do we get him back where he belongs?" Ralph continued non-stop.

At noon, we drove to Dexter's wharf so Ralph could see Sam. He was swimming about but once he saw us walk out on the wharf; he swam over looking for food.

"Sam, what are you doing over here?" Ralph asked as he fed the swan. "You had us worried." When the food was gone, Sam swam back to the safety of the open water.

As we headed home, we tried to comprehend what caused Sam to undertake such a long, arduous trip. From our aerial photograph of Marion, Ralph measured the distance from the Old Landing to the Weweantic River—it had been an eight mile swim for Sam. What made him do this? Was he trying to escape the hunters in Sippican Harbor? Was the trip his answer to a migration urge? The answer to those questions will forever be a mystery to us.

"Remember the man at the Old Landing last summer who told us that he had seen Sam in the Weweantic River before." Ralph recalled. "We didn't believe him. We were sure it was another swan that he had seen. Well, we now know that it probably was Sam!"

In the late afternoon, we returned to Dexter's wharf with Sam's supper. Seeing us, he quickly swam towards us. To the north side of the wharf, there was a small sandy beach so we tried to coax Sam out on shore. Although he did swim to the water's edge, he would not leave the safety of the water, preferring his supper tossed out to him. For the next week, we fed Sam twice a day; he stayed in the water and we tossed food to him as he floated close to shore.

By the end of that week, Sam felt secure enough in his new surroundings to walk onto the beach to eat. Two days before Christmas, the cold deepened and ice formed along the shore. We went back to feeding him from the wharf. It wasn't an ideal feeding arrangement for Sam.

"I have a solution," Ralph announced the next night. "Down cellar there is a large piece of foam insulation board. I'll make a floating collar for a feeding dish. By attaching a string to a corner of it, we can float the dish out to Sam and then retrieve it once he's finished eating."

"I've a glass pie plate that would be an ideal feeding dish," I added enthusiastically. "It's not too deep yet wide enough for Sam to place his bill into it to eat. Let's get busy. If we make it tonight, we can serve

Sam Christmas breakfast from a plate. Do you think he will eat from it?"

"It will be interesting to see how he reacts. We'll have to bring fresh water to put in the dish. That will make it easier for Sam to eat."

Christmas morning was cloudy, calm and cold. The weak sun was trying to push through the cloud layer without success. We ate quickly and traveled to Dexter's wharf. We did not meet a single car. It was as though we were the only two people left in town. We found Sam floating close to shore as if waiting for our arrival.

"Good morning, Sam. Merry Christmas," I called as though he could understand me. Without hesitation, he swam towards us. He had adjusted so well to his new surroundings that we wondered if he planned to stay there all winter. We hoped not for we knew the river would freeze completely with the next Arctic cold front from Canada. How would we feed Sam once the ice forced him farther and farther out towards the open bay?

"Sam, we have something new for you to try." Ralph said as he added bread to the empty dish. He lowered the foam collar cradling the dish with the bread in it to the water's surface, then added fresh water. "Come eat, Sam."

Sam stopped his forward motion when he noticed the floating dish; slowly the wings came up, the feathers on his head and neck fluffed up. Sam's movements became distrustful of the piece of white floating foam. It mattered not there was food in it! As the dish approached him, Sam cautiously backed away from it.

"Sam, it's okay; there is nothing to be afraid of," Ralph said.

Tentatively Sam swam towards the floating dish, his wings fully raised. Ralph and I watched silently. We observed that Sam seemed torn between hunger and the fear of what danger may lurk within the strange thing floating towards him. Finally, hunger drove him towards the food in the dish. Inching closer, Sam stretched his long neck, reached into the dish, snatched a piece of bread, and drew his head back with the speed of a blink of an eye! When nothing dire happened to him, he began to eat from the floating dish. Then he discovered there was fresh water in the dish. He noisily slurped the water, raised his head and let the water trickle down his long neck.

"He likes drinking fresh water from a dish," I whispered.

"Good boy, Sam," Ralph praised the swan. "Now we can feed you when the ice forms and you can't come ashore. We will push the dish over the ice to you."

"Shall we try to give Sam some cracked corn in his dish?" Ralph asked when we returned home. "The cracked corn has more nutritional value than bread."

"Maybe Sam won't eat it." I countered.

"We won't know unless we offer it to Sam."

To our surprise Sam ate the cracked corn without hesitation and seemed to relish it. We both were pleased, as we felt the calories in the corn were better for him.

For the next two days, feeding Sam was ordinary. However, when we arrived to give Sam breakfast on the third day, we could not find him. A thick layer of fog silently drifted over the smooth slate gray water. Cleveland's Light foghorn at the west entrance to the Cape Cod Canal moaned in the stillness, but there was no graceful swan swimming about.

"Now where has he gone?" Ralph asked in exasperation. "Do you suppose he has gone farther down the river?"

"He wouldn't be able to get very far as the ice is closing the open water fast. Let's check Dexter Beach; it's just around the bend. He could navigate down the middle of the river to get there," I said. Sam was not there.

"Do you think Sam is swimming back to Sippican Harbor?" I asked. "Maybe some natural involuntary impulse encourages him to move again."

"It would be an easy solution to the problem of how to get him back where he belongs," Ralph answered. "I really don't want to try to capture him because I think it would terrify Sam. He'd be so frightened by the ordeal he would never come to us again."

At noon we checked both places again hoping to find him but without success. At three o'clock, I made my final check of the day. Sam had disappeared again!

Early the next morning we began searching again. Our first stop was the Old Landing, just in case he had returned during the night. Then we headed to Dexter's wharf on the chance that he might have returned to the river. Not finding him there, we searched along all the outer reaches of the Weweantic River and the eastern shore of Sippican Harbor. When we did not locate him, we went home to start the Saturday chores.

"He'll show up in one of the two places he's been fed recently," Ralph stated with assurance.

Mid-morning we went downtown. When we reached the Old Landing, we drove in for one more check.

"I see him! Look off Tabor's dock," Ralph's voice was jubilant. Sure enough, down the mid channel of the harbor came the familiar large white swan looking like a victorious knight of old returning home.

"How about that! Sam's back!" I was jubilant and relieved to have our favorite swan back at the Old Landing. "What do you suppose prompted him to take such a long trip? What told him he should come back?"

"I'm afraid only Sam knows the answers to your questions and he isn't talking" Ralph answered. "He must be hungry."

When Sam reached the boat ramp, we were ready to serve him his breakfast. He swam up to the floating dish and ate hungrily. Here was a bird that needed his calories after such a long swim.

"Now you stay here," Ralph instructed the full, contented swan. Glad to have Sam back where he belonged, we headed on our way.

Chapter Six

THE SECOND WINTER

After his Weweantic River adventure, Sam stayed around the Old Landing. Within two weeks' time, ice formed over the shallow reaches of the inner harbor. We were back to feeding Sam in the brook behind Daggett House.

"I dread having Sam spend another winter here," Ralph said one afternoon as we watched the swan bathe. "There isn't much open water for him to swim away from a charging dog. I wish there was a safer place."

"How would we get Sam to move to another feeding spot?" I asked. "Picking him up would destroy his fragile trust in us. All we can do is make frequent visits to check on him throughout the day. He has survived many years on his own."

All our worrying was for naught; Sam wisely chose the prudent winter home. One mid-January morning we arrived at the Old Landing to find the harbor covered with ice and Sam nowhere in sight. We made an unsuccessful search of the western shoreline for the missing swan.

"Hammett Cove has open water. He could be there but out of sight" Ralph suggested. "Let's see if we can see him from the campgrounds' beach."

However, solid ice covered the cove as far as we could see. "I don't see him. Do you?" I asked studying the many ice-covered rocks at the mouth of the cove.

"He may be there but hidden by a rock or be in an inlet and out of sight."

"We could walk along the shore from here," I suggested.

"That's not possible because of the large ice slabs that litter the shoreline. One of us could fall, possibly break a leg. Then we'd have a bigger problem," Ralph reasoned. "Let's visit the Fire Chief, he may know of an access road that we can use."

"There's a road on a waterfront estate that will take you right down to the shore," he told us. "I'm sure no one will mind your going there just to look for Sam."

From our vantage point on the private road we saw several large white lumps scattered over the mostly ice bound cove. Most had rocks protruding through them. However, there was one lump that was smoother and rounder than the others.

"It's Sam!" I exclaimed as I looked through the binoculars. "He's sound asleep with his head tucked under his wing." As we watched, Sam's head popped up and he looked about his ice-enshrouded world. He stretched his wings; first moving one wing straight out, then slowly back toward his tail and finally folding it into its resting position; then he stretched the other wing.

"Do you think he's stuck to the ice?" I asked.

Answering my unheard question, Sam stood and stretched his wings in the cold morning breeze. As he flapped his wings, his feet slipped on the ice and he actually moved forward a few feet towards the open water.

"Our next problem is how are we going to feed him," Ralph said with concern. "We can't reach him from here. The ice extends quite a distance from shore. It will be a long and difficult walk along the western shore from the campground beach but it can be done."

"Well, if we must do it, we'll do it," I answered. One way or the other, I knew we would see that Sam got the needed meal.

It was then that Ralph's problem solving engineering talent took charge. I always marveled at how he could study a problem and quickly come up with a possible solution. Along the western shore was an old rock retaining wall with the water flowing freely by it.

"If we can get permission to walk across the land on the other shore, we can reach Sam," Ralph suggested. "Let's go see George again. Maybe he can tell us who the caretaker is for that estate."

An hour later, we were walking across the open field carrying Sam's feeding dish, fresh water, cracked corn, and bread. We squinted as the bright January sun glared off the unbroken snow cover on the field. When we reached the retaining wall, Sam was floating with his head underwater searching for food.

"Good morning, Sam," I called when his head came up. He looked in my direction as if to see who was there. "Come, Sam. We have your breakfast." Cautiously, he swam toward the familiar voice in the unfamiliar surroundings.

Fortunately, the tide was on its way out. Ralph climbed down the stone wall to the rocks below and placed the floating feeding dish in the water. I handed the cracked corn, bread and water to him; he quickly filled the dish.

As Ralph balanced on the icy rocks, Sam swam to the floating dish and ate, quickly emptying it. As Ralph moved to refill the dish, the cautious swan swam away. Ralph pushed the filled dish out a short distance and stood still. Sam returned to the dish to finish his meal.

With his hunger satisfied, Sam returned to the open water and began to preen. Ralph climbed up the wall and we quietly watched Sam bathe in the cold seawater. Soon, the cold biting north wind blowing across the open field sent us scurrying for home and hot coffee.

At first, we walked the mile distance twice a day to be sure that Sam had nourishment. To us, the area Sam had chosen for his winter home didn't have enough food to sustain a swan. Before long, we noticed Sam wasn't eating much food at one time; it was more like two small meals.

"Since it's harder for us to get here in the morning before work, let's try feeding him only in the afternoon," Ralph suggested one morning as we walked home from our visit with Sam. "We can leave some food for him to eat the next morning. We'll sprinkle the corn in the water, choosing a site that isn't too deep for Sam to easily reach down to the bottom to eat and shouldn't freeze-over during the night."

At the end of the afternoon feeding that day, we sprinkled the cracked corn as Sam watched. It was our hope that the next morning when we did not come with a fresh breakfast, Sam would remember where we left the corn. Although I could see the logic behind our decision of one feeding a day, I felt that I was letting Sam down by not appearing at breakfast time.

To Sam, it did not seem to matter at all. When we arrived the next afternoon, he was searching for food underwater. Seeing us, he swam quickly to the stone wall and waited for Ralph to place the feeding dish in front of him. Sam's head was in the dish before Ralph could pour the water.

While a very hungry Sam ate, I searched the place where we had left the corn the previous day but could not find any kernels sitting on the bottom. Sam must have remembered the corn and eaten it. My sense of guilt for not coming that morning faded.   As we left, we again sprinkled corn in the water for Sam's breakfast the next day.

At the beginning of February, we had a major snowstorm followed by a prolonged severe cold spell. The night temperatures dropped well below zero and hovered in the low single numbers during the day. The northwest wind howled and sent the powdery snow in mini squalls across the open fields.

As we prepared ourselves for a visit with Sam, we donned extra layers of clothing and protected our faces with scarves. The only exposed skin was around our eyes. As we trekked across the field, my warm breath fogged my glasses making it impossible to see where I was going. Reluctantly, I loosened the scarf; it was better to see and have a cold chin.

To our surprise, Sam still had open water in which to swim. Although the open water was shrinking in the severe cold, it still flowed freely by the stone wall. Sam seemed happy to see us, and quickly came to eat.

Except for the open water at the entrance of the cove, solid ice covered the harbor as far as I could see. With the absence of human activity, the emptiness of the cove was overwhelming.   Only the occasional loud cracks of ice expanding or contracting and the touchdown splash of a pair of Canada geese and the few ducks that shared Sam's winter home shattered the silence.   How desolate it was.

A few days later, as I searched my recipe file for a special treat to chase away the dreary winter blues, I found a Durgin-Park cornbread recipe.   We frequently dined at the famous restaurant at Boston's Faneuil Hall. Instead of the rolls most restaurants served, Durgin-Park placed a slab of fresh cornbread on the table to accompany their meals. Warm cornbread and hot tea were just the cure for our winter slump.

The next morning on a whim, I decided to take some cornbread for Sam. He loved cracked corn, why not cornbread? Sam hesitated when

I placed a single piece of cornbread in his dish. Sam knew there was something different about this yellow tidbit floating in his dish. To tempt him, I tossed a piece of the wheat bread next to it. Sam reached for the bread but ate both pieces. When I placed the second piece of cornbread in the dish, Sam gobbled it down. It was love at first bite!

This was the beginning of my cornbread baking for Ralph and Sam. However, I noticed Sam ate most of each double-batch of cornbread I baked twice a week.

By the third week in February, the severe cold was but a memory. The days were noticeably lengthening with a slight warming of the air.

One day Ralph suggested, "Let's make good use of the warmer temperature and feed Sam earlier today." It was a delightful late winter afternoon: bright sun, no wind, and a temperature in the mid-thirties. It was a day that whispered, ever so softly, that winter's hold on the land was weakening and spring was on the doorstep. I thoroughly enjoyed being outside on such a super day.

Sam was enjoying the fine day too. We found him floating in the calm water near a small spit of land that showed at low tide. With the slight warming of late winter, the ice line had receded. Nodding his head, he swam towards the point of land, telling us in his way that he wanted to eat there. As we walked across the ice, which at high tide had water under it but now rested on land at the low tide, our feet broke through and sank into the squishy muck below. Quickly, black mud caked our boots. As we worked our way out to him, Sam was already walking towards us, spattering mud showers as his large feet smacked the bare moist shore.

When we met, he grabbed my pant leg and held on securely while I stroked him for the first time in many days. He seemed to have missed the touching as much as me.

This was our first opportunity to visit with Sam on land since he decided to spend the winter in the cove. He stood very still and let me gently stroke his long neck, the upper back and underside.

Any touch of Sam's tail or his underside from his legs back brought forth a warning honk from him. I honored Sam's demands and never touched his tail. Although I often placed my cheek on his neck as I stroked him, Sam never nipped my face.

Finally, hunger took priority over stroking and Sam looked for his food. As his hunger lessened, he sat down to finish his meal in a leisurely fashion.

During the remainder of the winter confinement, we fed Sam on the little spit of land when the tide was right. Through these quiet winter days our relationship deepened and Sam's trust grew stronger. It was a very docile swan that placed his head in the crook of my arm and stood still while I stroked him. Somehow, the language barrier was overcome. Human and swan communicated through touches.

On another warm late winter day, Ralph and I prolonged our visit with Sam to observe more of his behavior. With the meal finished, Sam returned to the water. As we sat on a large rock at the water's edge, Sam began to bathe. To get the water on his back, he dipped his head sharply into the water, stretched his long neck to its fullest length and then quickly brought his head and neck up out of the water thus causing the water to travel down the lower neck and over the wings and back. This he did many times, then he swam to shallow water, stood up, and began to preen and oil his feathers.

Whenever we were puzzled by a behavior Sam displayed, I'd go to our local library to find an answer. If I couldn't find an answer at our local library, I'd go to the University of Massachusetts - Dartmouth Library for further research.

There I learned that Sam had an oil gland on his back at the base of his tail. It's the oil from that gland that protected him from the icy cold water that could be fatal if it reached his skin. He used this oil to coat his feathers, thus preventing water from seeping through them and reaching his body.

This was a time-consuming procedure and took his full attention. Sam reached around with his long neck, pinched the oil gland with his bill, and rubbed his chin over it gathering the oil. Then he turned and rubbed his chin back and forth over his chest feathers several times. He reached back to the oil gland again, then he rubbed his underside. Methodically, Sam oiled and preened every inch of his body.

Completing the job, he swam over to where we were sitting and floated in the calm water. He seemed to enjoy the late February warm sun as much as we did. We sat very still, closely observing the apparently contented swan.

"Sam is going to sleep!" Ralph whispered. As we watched, Sam's eyes closed, but only for a few seconds. Then they flickered open, studied us for a few seconds then closed again. Sam was dozing -"bird-napping" as he took quick peeks at us every so often.

"Sam's eye lids close from the bottom up!" I said with surprise. "They're covered with tiny feathers that look like fur." At the same time, I noticed Sam also had transparent inner eye lids that protected his eyes while he ate underwater. The inner lids moved from front to back over the eye as his head entered the surface of the water thus keeping the water from flooding his eye. How ingenious nature is, I thought.

Soon the sun fell below the western horizon and the chill crept back to claim the land. In the golden glow of sunset, a vee-shaped flock of geese flew over the frozen harbor searching for a spot to spend the night. Reluctantly, we gathered the food supplies, sprinkled corn for Sam's breakfast and headed home. We were elated with the show of trust Sam displayed by napping beside us. It had been a delightful afternoon.

As the days warmed, the ice began to melt along the shore. Sam appeared to be suffering from cabin fever. Every day he swam the length of the open shoreline as far as he could. On a trip to the Old

Landing one early afternoon, we saw him at the tip of Black Point. Still, solid ice prevented him from reaching the Old Landing boat ramp.

"Didn't make it back to the Old Landing today." Ralph greeted our feathered friend later that afternoon at the Hammett Cove feeding spot. "Sam, I'll be as happy as you when this ice disappears."

"It's March already," I said, "and still the ice holds."

One night a week later, a strong wind blew from the Northwest all night long. The next morning we decided to check the ice conditions from the Old Landing before heading to the cove. Driving into the Old Landing parking lot, we were surprised to find the harbor ice free. I could not see a single floe bobbing in the choppy water. It amazed me how so much ice could completely disappear overnight.

As we came around to the boat ramp, we were in for another surprise. There was Sam, busily preening his feathers in the bright sunshine as he waited for breakfast to come. How did he know we would feed him at the boat ramp that morning?

I felt a tinge of sadness over the end of Sam's Hammett Cove winter. In the solitude of the cove, we had learned much about this unique mute swan. It had been a good winter because Sam shared it with us. The three of us were no longer alone—barking dogs, noisy cars, and other sudden noises of civilization made it impossible to capture the special quietness of the cove. However, I was happy for Sam—now he had the whole harbor to explore.

Chapter Seven

AFTER HURRICANE GLORIA

Hurricane Gloria's howling winds blew over our area and was now headed toward the North Atlantic Ocean. We wondered what Sam's reaction would be when he saw us for the first time after the storm. Would he forgive our capturing him to make sure he was safe from Hurricane Gloria? Our last sighting of Sam was the morning after the hurricane when Ralph released him at the Old Landing.

When Sam did not show up for a noontime snack on the day after the hurricane, we launched our skiff to search for him. We hoped he would come to eat when he saw us, indicating his forgiveness. If he swam away, we'd need to re-establish the bond of trust shared with Sam.

Once on the water, our perspective of the hurricane damage changed. Looking back at the Old Landing, we saw a half-submerged sailboat dejectedly leaning against the side of the south wharf. When we came closer to the beached boats on the marsh surrounding Black Point, the devastation of the damaged sailboats hit home. One had a gaping hole in its starboard stern, just below the water line. Another looked as though some giant hand had been pushing it through the water, tired of the chore and gently placed it on the marsh far from the high tide watermark. A sailboat with full sails set racing with the wind is a graceful sight. However, a beached sailboat looks gauche and awkward.

We located Sam swimming in the inlet to the east of Gravel Island, but as we approached he swam away! It appeared he was not going to quickly forgive our picking him up for his safety.

"Maybe he doesn't like having the boat coming towards him. I'll let you off on the north side of the island," Ralph suggested. "See if he will let you approach him from land. He may be more forgiving of you since you did not pick him up."

"Sam, Sam, corn bread" I called softly to Sam on the farther side. He watched me; his neck straight and taut, his body posture suggested a fight or flight appearance. Slowly, I took a step towards him. To my dismay, he swam in the opposite direction. The fragile trusting bond between us was shattered. However, he did not swim far, just what he probably considered a safe distance from me.

"Come, Sam," I called as I climbed on a rock and placed the filled dish in the water beside it. "Cornbread is served," I coaxed as I pushed his dish a few feet from the rock, but Sam kept his distance. I left the rock and stepped back ten feet. A very tentative swan inched his way towards the floating dish while constantly watching me. Hungrily, he ate while I stood still on the island.

"How's it going?" Ralph inquired from the skiff.

"He's eating his cornbread," I quietly called over my shoulder being torn between letting Ralph know Sam was eating while not wanting to startle the swan. Even my soft voice sent Sam immediately swimming away from his dish.

I could not coax Sam back to his dish. With his hunger partially satisfied now, it seemed fear of capture ruled his reactions to the world around him. Pleased that at least Sam did come to his dish to eat, I returned to the skiff.

"Sam ate some cornbread, but he seemed spooked by my voice."

"We knew this might happen," Ralph answered. "At least he still wants our food."

During the next few days, Sam occasionally came to the Old Landing for food. He refused to come up on the beach to eat, and we had to be content to float his filled food dish out to him.

Slowly, painfully slowly, his trust in us returned. A month passed before Sam swam to the water's edge to eat. It was a few weeks more before he walked up the beach to his dish. While his trust in us was rebuilding, we made sure to keep our voices low and our movements slow. We had sorely missed the close, personal contact with that special bird. What we longed for most was to stroke him again as he stood besides us. That would tell us that Sam really forgave us for picking him up.

Words proved inadequate to express our joy when, a month later, Sam stood quietly as I stroked him from his chin, down his long neck to his tummy. He even accepted my touch on his back. Sam forgave us!

Chapter Eight

OLD LANDING WINTER

The year of 1986, the third winter of caring for our favorite swan, arrived with a bitter north wind but no snow cover. Sam had open water for the first nine days of the New Year. When the ice did form, it was in a different pattern from the pervious year. It formed a line from Black Point to Knowlton House. Sam (on the north side of the ice barrier) was confined to the Old Landing area. However, the water around the wharf and the beach flowed freely so he came ashore to eat.

One very cold windy afternoon our granddaughter, Danielle, joined us to feed Sam. She was not intimidated by his size as some children were and loved to feed him. The strong wind noisily whipped the high flying flag at the Old Landing and pushed us down to the beach.

"Can I feed Sam?" Danielle asked in a muffled voice through the scarf covering her lower face. With the hood of her snowsuit covering her forehead, all I saw of my granddaughter was a pair of large brown eyes and a rosy red nose.

I placed a piece of bread on Danielle's mitten-covered hand and she offered it to the swan. To her disappointment, Sam would not take the cornbread from the bulky mitten.

"No, Danielle, don't take your mittens off," I said as another blast of wind whipped around us. "Why don't you get in the car?" I suggested when Danielle began to shiver. Without protest, she ran to the car. Although Sam ate heartily, he seemed to relish the tepid fresh water I gave him. After each sip, he raised his head skyward and slowly swallowed the water, appearing to savor each drop.

Sam quickly ate and entered the water. He had a thick layer of down beneath the sleek outer feathers that kept his body warm but his feet and bill were exposed to the biting wind. We had noticed that in severe cold weather Sam's bill changed color, from a light orange-red to a deeper rosy red-orange hue. Taking a sip of salt water, he pushed himself free from the shallow bottom and paddled away from shore.

"See where he's going? Right between the wharf and the barge," Ralph said. "Danielle, Sam's a wise old bird. He knows where to go to get out of the wind. Maybe he plans to sleep there tonight."

"I'm glad I'm not Sam's wife, Grandpa," she answered. "I wouldn't want to sleep there."

While the spot offered protection from the strong wind, it was where the ice would first form as the temperature dropped. I wondered if Sam knew that. Some super cold winter nights, we left Sam in the water only to find him up on the ice some distance from shore the next morning. We had no idea how Sam decided where to sleep. Did he move farther from shore as the ice formed near him? Or did he sense where ice was likely to form and move away from the area so as not to become stuck?

The next morning, Sam was floating at the further end of the barge, out beyond the ice that closed his access to shore.

"I'll try to throw cornbread to him," Ralph suggested. "He'll have to go without his corn and water this morning." The first piece slid across the ice right to Sam. He ate it quickly. The second piece stopped short of Sam, but he stretched his long neck and reached it.

"Darn," Ralph cursed when a piece of cornbread stopped far short of Sam. The next piece landed far beyond Sam's reach. After a while, the cornbread pieces dropped close enough for Sam to eat them. We noticed he did not devour the food like a starving swan.

"Every gull in the harbor is coming to eat," Ralph said as more and more gulls circled noisily overhead, waiting for a chance to grab some of Sam's breakfast. "That's it!" Ralph fumed as one gull intercepted a piece of cornbread in midair. "Let's stop. There's no reason to feed the gulls. They can easily fly to open water to feed." We waited out the gulls. Finally, they flew off. Then we finished tossing breakfast to the one who really needed our food.

Sam was about twenty-two to twenty-four years old, middle age for a mute swan (their life expectancy in the wild was twenty to thirty years but in captivity they could live to be forty plus years old). Sam, not being able to fly, lived in semi-captivity. Mute swans do not have any natural enemies; high wires are the greatest threat when they fly.

We calculated his age from talking to people who had known Sam previous to the early 1980's. Some met him when they first moved to town. Others met him when they first moored their boat in Sippican Harbor and Sam came to their boat looking for food. One woman who lived along the shore recalled Sam visiting during her daughter's home wedding reception. Each person provided us a year to help us estimate Sam's unknown age.

By late afternoon, the bright January sun melted the thin ice around the Old Landing. The ebb and flow of the tide pushed the remaining soft ice aside enough for Sam to come to the beach.

"Sam has ice droplets on his back," Ralph said. "I wish we could take him home with us."

"Sam would not like it one bit!" I replied. We sure would be pleased having him under cover in a building. It was in wintertime that we worried the most as Sam, flightless, had to cope with snowstorms, ice, and severely cold temperatures. Some winter mornings we drove through freshly fallen snow to reach the Old Landing to feed the swan. There, Sam would be patiently waiting for us at the boat ramp, in the brook or at the boat yard.

Arriving the next morning, we found Sam asleep on the ice across from the north dock; in the area we called "Sam's Lookout." Ralph and I coined special names for all the Old Landing areas that Sam frequents. Sam raised his head in answer to our calls, stood up and flapped his wings. It looked as if he wanted to get airborne, but of course that was forever impossible.

"He's not ready to eat," Ralph said when the swan began to preen his feathers.

"I'll come back later to give him breakfast."

When I returned, Sam was in the same spot and still not ready to eat. By midmorning, Sam was in the water. Seeing me, he swam to the north dock.

"Come, Sam," I called as I dropped goldfish-shaped crackers in front of him, coaxing him into open water between the north and south wharves where he would be out of the cold wind. There he ate the tossed cornbread and crackers.

After picking Danielle up from nursery school, we stopped to see Sam. He was still floating between the wharves. It was easy to understand why Sam was still there. The water was calm and the sun gave meager warmth to the cold atmosphere.

"Can I throw some crackers to Sam?" Danielle asked.

"You can toss a few crackers." I answered, handing her the bag of crackers. "Grandpa didn't get to visit with Sam earlier. I want Sam to be hungry enough to stay here until Grandpa arrives." As she tossed the crackers, Sam expressed his happiness by wiggling his tail. He churned the water with his feet, creating a floating cloud of mud in the shallow water that hid the bottom.

By late afternoon, Sam had moved to the south side of the south wharf. While thin ice was forming between the barge and dock, there was open water at the southeast corner. A thin crust of ice covered the harbor, thin enough to react to the gentle movement of the water below. I loved to watch this gentle rippling of the ice.

Because the tide was high, Ralph climbed down the side of the wharf to place Sam's dish of cracked corn in front of him.

A few days later, Sam was iced-in at Sam's Lookout, too far away to toss food to him. The ice separating us was dark, suggesting that it was still thin enough for the water underneath to show ominously through the surface.

"Sam could plow through this ice if he was hungry," Ralph stated. "Maybe the full sunshine will be enough to melt the ice so he can come to eat by noon."

"I hope he doesn't choose to stay there," I said.

"If solid ice forms, he'll have to walk himself over here. I can't see us walking the marsh twice a day. Not when we know he can walk the short distance to here."

I returned several times to check on Sam's whereabouts just in case he decided to come for breakfast. By midmorning, he had pushed his way sixty yards to the south dock. There was a definite slushy crooked track through the soft ice that showed Sam's route. However, he had already turned around and was now sitting in his own trail fifteen to twenty feet from me, facing northward. I tossed some cornbread to him but he did not make the slightest effort to reach it. Obviously, Sam was not hungry!

By noontime, he had turned about again, moved past the south dock and was sitting in a very small patch of water. His body gave off enough heat to keep the water from freezing under him. There he sat, surrounded by ice as far as the eye could see; one lone mute swan under a weak January sun filtered by high clouds, surveying his icy kingdom. He made no effort to reach us.

"He has to be hungry!" I said. "He's had nothing to eat all day."

"Remember, this is winter," Ralph answered. The metabolism of wild swans slows down in the winter to compensate for when their normal food is scarce. They live off the body fat they stored up during the summer and autumn. If we did not feed Sam, that's how he'd survive when icebound. Besides, he's not using very many calories just sitting on the ice."

In the late afternoon we found Sam in the same spot. "Do you suppose he's stuck to the ice?" I asked. "It's not like him to miss a meal."

"He can't be; he has moved about since morning. He should be hungry enough to come for food."

We blinked the car lights, hoping to pique Sam's interest enough to come for supper. Then Ralph got out of the car, called to the swan, and shook the bread bag in his outstretched hand so Sam could see it. Finally, Sam pushed himself through the thin ice to the end of the south dock.

Ralph lowered the foam collar for the dish to the soft ice below. Then he climbed down the icy stones to place Sam's dish, filled with cracked corn, in the waiting collar. Ralph realized he was not close enough to the water's surface to be able to place the dish safely into the holder. There wasn't a lower ledge for Ralph to climb down so he could reach the collar. Sam pushed himself through the ice, finally reaching us. He seemed puzzled by the empty foam ring. Ralph threw some loose cracked corn on the ice near Sam. He managed to eat just a few kernels. Was he afraid his bill would freeze to the ice or was it too difficult to eat the corn one kernel at a time?

When he finished eating, we returned to the car and waited to see what Sam's plans were for the night. First, he bathed in the icy water. We shivered for him! Completing his bath, Sam pushed himself through the soft ice, back to the same spot where he spent the afternoon. As we watched, he climbed up on the ice and pushed himself away from the open water. We finally had an answer to one of our questions about Sam. He did move away from the edge of the ice when he retired for the night thus reducing the chances of being caught in newly forming ice.

We recalled one unusually cold winter many years ago. Our friend Nelson received a call from someone claiming Sam was stuck to the ice off the Old Landing. The caller said the swan had been in the same spot since the previous afternoon. Since men had been ice fishing on the frozen harbor, Nelson decided to come to Sam's rescue. He walked out on the solidly frozen ice. Just as Nelson reached him, Sam stood up, gave a threatening honk, lowered his head, and started walking forward with his wings flapping. It wasn't a friendly greeting; Sam didn't appreciate the effort of his would-be rescuer one bit. Nelson retreated, with Sam following along still flapping his wings. Sam does know how to cope with the difficulties of winter. Some winter mornings we wondered if Sam was stuck in ice, only to wait awhile and see him move.

"He's sitting at the east end of the barge," Ralph said. "He's using the barge and south dock as wind breakers." The swan, sitting in a very small patch of open water, looked lonely and small against the expanse of ice, the huge rusty barge, and the wharf. Sam's wise choices when faced by survival difficulties always amazed me.

"You can do it," Ralph encouraged the swan. Sam tried to reach the corner of the south dock using his body as an icebreaker. The ice held solid and unyielding under his weight. Repeatedly, Sam tried but failed to push himself through the ice.

That morning, with the higher tide, Ralph was able to place the food dish on the ice surface below the dock but now Sam could not make the connection. Sam had a breakfast of tossed bread. Although he did not eat as much as we felt he should, he appeared satisfied with what we threw to him. We wanted Sam to eat the cracked corn from his dish because we felt it fortified him better to cope with the severe cold spell. However, we were very thankful to get any food to him.

We experienced three days of mild weather before winter returned on January 14 with strong gusty winds and a temperature of ten degrees by early morning. We located Sam sound asleep on the ice twenty feet from the end of the boatyard dock, with his head tucked snugly under his wing. The brisk north wind ruffled his outer feathers but we knew Sam did not feel the biting cold wind as he slept.

"Sam, Sam," I called out once, twice and three times before Sam's head popped up. The ice was now thick enough to support his heavy weight although he was lying very close to its edge. He stretched his body from sleep; first extending his left wing and foot and then the right wing and foot. Sam slowly pushed himself into the cold blue water surrounding the wooden dock and swam toward shore.

The boatyard owners had placed four underwater fans to churn the water on cold nights so the ice could not form and damage the pilings. This was the ideal location for Sam's winter home—an area of open water in which to swim, bathe, and exercise. While those probably were the reasons he liked it, we liked it because it was easier to feed Sam there twice a day. "Breakfast is served," I called to Sam as he paddled toward us. The early morning sun fell on us, dispelling ever so slightly the bone-chilling air. The large boats on their winter skids protected us from the north wind. In spite of the unusually cold temperature the night before, the water in front of the rocky boat ramp was ice free. Sam arrived for breakfast wearing a covering of ice droplets from his short swim. After gulping a few pieces of tossed cornbread, Sam stopped eating.

"Why isn't he eating?" questioned Ralph. "He acted so hungry when he first came." Sam's sudden lack of appetite puzzled us.

Sam rubbed his bill over his body feathers. Then he put his bill in the saltwater and tried to blow bubbles. Next, he rubbed his bill on his body again. Then he dipped his bill in the water once more.

"I know what the problem is," Ralph announced after careful observation. "The small openings on his bill are freezing up." Sam had two small openings on his upper bill about the size of human nostrils and they were icing over in the ten-degree air temperature!

We coaxed Sam ashore to drink the tepid water we brought. As he slowly walked up the icy shore, I poured the water into his dish. A small vapor cloud formed over it. Sam hesitated cautiously for a split second before taking a sip. As he noisily slurped the water, his bill made a soft clicking sound. His actions seemed to express complete satisfaction as he held his head high and savored the tepid water as it trickled down his neck. An element of slow, unhurried movement in Sam told us he was content. There was no need to rush the meal; tepid water must be fully savored on such a cold morning.

Then Sam began to eat the bread in his dish. Although he ate some of the cracked corn, he did not eat as much as we thought he should. Maybe like some people, he was not hungry when he first awoke from a long night's sleep. Once finished with eating, he returned to the water as we picked up the leftover food.

A short distance from shore, Sam stopped for his customary after-breakfast bath. Down his head went into the cold water. He stretched his neck straight out and quickly brought it up through the water's surface, sending water coursing down his long neck, over his back and onto his wings that were held tightly to his body. A wiggle of the tail sent the last of the water off in a spray of droplets. A couple of more dips in the water, then Sam stood in the shallow water and fanned his wings in the cold air, tossing water droplets in every direction. Then Sam swam to the spot where we found him asleep, climbed up on the ice and began to oil his feathers. Next, he sat on the ice, shook his left foot to get rid of any water droplets on it, and tucked the foot snugly into the feathers lining the left side of his body. Then he did the same to his right foot. Thus, he settled down to pass a humdrum winter day.

Sam settled down to pass a humdrum winter day

The boatyard owners had placed four underwater fans to churn the water on cold nights so the ice could not form and damage the pilings.

Chapter Nine

UNEXPECTED VISITORS

"Sam has visitors," Ralph announced excitedly when he came in for lunch on January 16. "There are two swans swimming with him!"

"What's Sam's reaction to the company?" I asked, remembering the stories we had heard of how he chased away any swan that landed in the harbor.

"Everything was peaceful!" he reassured me. "Each had its head underwater, eating when I arrived. When Sam came to eat, the other two watched but didn't swim closer. They ate the bread I tossed to them but refused to eat the goldfish-shaped crackers."

"Is it a pair?"

"No. One is an adult and the other is small enough to be last spring's cygnet. Come on, I want you to see them. No telling how long Sam will let them stay. He might decide he doesn't want any visitors and evict them."

At the boatyard, we found the three swans swimming gracefully around the dock. Their white feathers, striking against the vivid deep-blue water, reflected the bright sunshine as the azure sky completed the picturesque scene.

The larger swan, about Sam's size, had a black knob that was smaller than his that helped us identify it as possibly a female. To me, the little white swan looked to be a cygnet as there was no knob; its bill was buff-colored and rounded on top, with a slightly pointed tip. It had all the appearances of a cygnet, including awkward adolescence mannerisms. It was impossible to determine the sex of this swan; it was just too young.

"I'm surprised by Sam's acceptance of their presence," I said, puzzled by what I saw. "Maybe it's because one is female and the other an adolescent."

To us, Sam claimed proprietary rights as strong as any third or fourth generation town resident. We were pleased he allowed the two swans to stay long enough for me to see them. Another possible reason for Sam's ready acceptance of them was the fact it was winter.

"If they were an adult pair," Ralph said, "I'm sure Sam would have evicted them immediately."

Mute swans often flock together during this season when there is a limited amount of open water. These were educated guesses on our part; only Sam knew the real reason for his tolerance.

When Sam swam to us to eat, the two swans stayed back.

"They're eating bread," Ralph said, "which means people have fed them at one time or another." However, they obviously had not experienced the close human contact that Sam shared with us since they remained at a safe distance. After the bread was gone, we stayed to observe the three swans until work duties compelled us to leave.

Returning at four-thirty that afternoon, we did not find the swans at the boat yard.

"Look at who's swimming together," I said in happy surprise when we saw Sam and the adult swan from the Old Landing wharf. Sam and the larger swan were to the south of the north wharf, having pushed their way through the soft ice. They had already turned about and were headed back to the boatyard. "Where do you suppose the little swan is now?"

"There it is," Ralph pointed to the south of the Old Landing area. Struggling, the little swan valiantly pushed its way through the ice following in the larger swans' trail, far behind Sam and his new friend.

"Did you hear that?" I asked. Listening, we heard faint peeps from the little swan as it passed the wharf where we stood. "She must be calling for the other two to wait for her. Either they don't hear or they're choosing to ignore her pleading calls."

While it pleased me to see Sam and the larger swan develop a relationship, I was sad that it was at the expense of the little swan. Although both swans had arrived together, now the cygnet appeared to be rejected by Sam and its former traveling companion. Apparently, it did not understand the situation and doggedly tried to stay with the other swans.

Back at the boat yard, Sam came ashore to eat while the other two swam closer to us to eat the tossed bread.

"Watch this," I said throwing a couple of pieces of cornbread to them. Eagerly, they stretched their long necks to pick it up. However, once they had the cornbread in their bills, they dropped it! "They don't know it's good to eat." I wondered if it was the coarse texture of the cornbread that made them refuse to eat it.

"Sam loves his cornbread so much, I'm not sure he'd want to share it," Ralph answered. The visitors watched Sam eat but they did not swim any closer to us.

"We should name the two visitors," I suggested. "We can't keep calling them big and little swan. How about Sally or Nancy for the female?" Somehow, we thought neither name fit the larger swan. "What about Samantha?" I offered. "Sam and Samantha sound good together should they become a pair."

"That fits her," Ralph answered. "I like the name Little One for the smallest swan." Thus, we named our first two swans. Sam already had the name of Samson when we met him. However, he also had two other names. The men at the boatyard called him Billy while others knew him as Swanie. Of the three names, we thought Samson fit this unique bird best and all we did was shorten it to Sam.

Slowly the signs of impending nightfall began; the boatyard activity halted as the men parked the forklift and locked the boat-shed doors for the night. A worker walked over the wooden dock, his footsteps echoing loudly. He flipped the switches to turn on the underwater fans to churn the water to prevent ice from forming around the dock pilings. The boatyard nightlights flashed on signaling the end of another workday. One by one the workers got into their trucks and drove off. Presently, we were alone with the swans in the gathering darkness. Soon, the deepening cold penetrated our clothes and chilled us to the bone. Although we didn't want to leave, it was time to go home.

"Will we find three swans in the morning?" Ralph wondered aloud as we left the swans swimming peacefully in the semi-darkness. "Sippican Harbor may be a stopover point on a longer journey for Samantha and Little One. They are here because ice has probably forced them from where they were," Ralph continued. "Will they be content with the small patch of open water for the duration of the winter?"

"They're still together," Ralph said when we found the swans at the boat yard the next morning. With each feeding session, they came closer to us, although they did not walk up on shore to eat. Ever so slowly, they were adapting to their new home.

Breakfast ended quickly and we left wondering if the three birds would spend the day together. The morning temperature, in the low twenties, felt warm after the single digit temperatures of the past few days. Where would the swans be at noon? Would Sam be alone again?

At noon, we found only Sam and Samantha swimming in the mid-channel water where the tidal current and bright January sun had melted the thinner ice. Along the shore the ice held firm. We could not feed the swans at the Old Landing boat ramp.

"I don't see Little One. Do you?" Ralph asked, searching the area with the binoculars.

"Do you suppose the other two have evicted it?" I answered a question with a question.

"Let's see if she's at Island wharf," Ralph suggested. We did not find her there.

"Little One doesn't seem strong enough to survive the winter on her own" I said, expressing my concern for her. "She's so small and thin! It seemed as though she ate only at the consent of the older swans."

"Yes, but we made sure she ate as well as they," Ralph answered comfortingly. "I hope she finds another human friend wherever she's gone. Otherwise she'll starve to death."

We shuddered at the prospects of Little One trying to fend for herself in an icebound environment. Her departure, whether forced or chosen, saddened us.

For the next few days feeding time settled into a quiet routine as Sam and Samantha ate their meals at the boat yard. The relationship between the two swans deepened. There was lots of bubble blowing, head dipping and nodding between the two, all signs of acceptance and bonding with mute swans.

"Our wishes for Sam to have a friend," Ralph said, "have been fulfilled." We delighted in Sam's unexpected good fortune of a 'girlfriend' falling from out of the blue!

"Sam seems as pleased with Samantha's presence as we are," I added.

Two winters earlier, during a severely cold February, a large flock of mutes gathered in the thickly settled area of the Wareham River where open water remained. After several people told us about the flock, we decided to go see them.

What a sight! Everywhere I looked I saw swans in front of me! As I walked down the bank with a large loaf of bread in hand, thirty-five hungry swans moved towards me as a single unit. Instinctively, they knew I was carrying food. As I knelt down on the ice lacing the snow covered shore, the hungriest swans gathered around me. Soon they were oblivious to my presence as they concentrated on eating the bread tossed to them before a neighboring bird grabbed it.

While the younger members of the flock approached us, the older and wiser swans kept their distance. Enchanted by the opportunity to study other mutes so closely, we carefully watched the interaction between the swans.

The interplay between flock members appeared much like what occurs in a gathering of thirty people. Some swans went about their own business with no thought of their neighbors. Others submissively bowed to the wishes of aggressive flock members. Some ventured forth until given a warning nip from an objecting neighbor. Even a swan flock has its tyrannical, overbearing, pacifist and timid members.

Among the gathering of swans were ducks, geese and aggressive gulls ready to share the bread. My large loaf did not last long.

"Do you think Sam would like to have the small swan sitting over there?" I asked Ralph, pointing out a small female.

"I chose that one for him also," Ralph laughed at our picking out the same swan for Sam. The big question was, would Sam like our choice?

She sat all by herself, patiently waiting for a piece of bread to come her way. She had a princess quality about her! She was too delicate to fight her way through the pushing and shoving mutes fighting for my next piece of bread.

"She'd be a good choice," Ralph added. "She has a regal look about her like Sam. Too bad we don't know how he'd react to another swan."

Back then, we had no way of knowing what Sam would do. If Sam rejected the female, could she find her way back to this river? After careful consideration, we decided to leave the little female with the flock. Sam would not miss what he had not known.

We visited with the Wareham flock several times before the end of February, when the warming atmosphere sent the entire flock dispersing for the coming breeding season. I wanted to follow each pair on its journey to their nesting site and to see where the adolescents chose to spend the summer that year.

Each winter since then, I've looked for a large gathering of swans on the Wareham River. They have never returned in such numbers. In recent winters I found only a dozen or fewer swans wintering there.

"What a delightful day," I proclaimed on the foggy Sunday. By noon, the fog lifted some and a hazy sun shone. It felt like spring with a temperature of forty-four degrees! Each January we have a thaw that is as welcomed as the first robin of spring. The few days of moderate temperatures is a prediction of warmer spring days to come just when the cold is deepest and the winter most depressing. This was a slight hint that spring was preparing for her return engagement upon the frozen land. However, we knew the bitter cold would return with the swift passage of an Arctic cold front straight from the Hudson Bay area of Canada. We New Englanders call them 'Alberta Clippers'.

That morning, for the first time, Samantha walked on shore and ate from Sam's dish. We held our breaths, waiting for Sam's reaction to having another swan eat his corn! He stood, waited for Samantha to lift her head from the dish, and then he ate from the dish.

"Sam's in love! He's sharing his dish," I said softly.

Quietly, we watched as first one and then the other ate cracked corn. A minute or two later, both had their bills in the dish at the same time. However, Samantha still refused to eat any of the homemade cornbread that Sam relished so much.

Samantha was beautiful. Watching her fan the air with her stretched wings, I marveled at their size and the power they possessed to lift a bird of her size into the air. I could only surmise what it looked like, for I had never seen a swan fly. A friend who had seen swans in flight said I would never forget my first sighting of a swan flying. So far, that joy eluded me, even with all the swans I had seen in the Wareham River. Not a one of them flew while I was there.

With breakfast finished, the swans returned to the water and started to bathe. Soon the courting began: first Sam dipped his bill into the water and blew bubbles, then Samantha returned the gesture and before long, both were blowing bubbles like crazy. Next they swam towards each other and came together; their heads high with their bills and chests touching, forming a perfect heart shape silhouette. Aha, love! Gracefully, without any visual indication, they smoothly glided about so they swam side by side in complete unison like a pair of graceful ballet dancers—a perfect picture of symmetry and love.

Suddenly, Sam stretched his long neck high and trumpeted. "Wow," exclaimed a surprised Ralph. "He's never done that before."

Samantha quickly answered with a trumpet of her own. Between the trumpets, the swans communicated with low soft purrs that sounded much like people quietly clearing their throats. I read that swans use this soft voice to communicate with one another. The trumpet call was a courting voice. We sat there, enthralled by the display of courtship that lasted about ten minutes before they silently glided away. Sam led the way majestically with his wings raised slightly and his head held high, seeming to nobly proclaim that the female following was his.

"Sam's one happy bird" Ralph said jubilantly. "Maybe we'll see cygnets this spring."

That was another swan wish I held: to see Sam's cygnets. A few people who knew Sam years ago told us he did have a mate and cygnets one year. However, the mate flew away when winter settled in and never returned. That's the story we have been told but wonder if it is really true. Mute swans mate for life and rarely choose a second mate on the death of the first one. Since Sam's long swim to the Weweantic River, I don't disallow anything about this unique swan's escapades.

Sam's life had sure taken a turn for the better with the arrival of Samantha. I wondered if he experienced any form of happiness or serenity with the arrival of a female. If only we could communicate heart to heart!

"I don't believe it!" I said a week later when we discovered the small white swan bobbing in the choppy blue-green water off the dock at Tabor. Just when we convinced ourselves that Little One was safely in a place where she had food, here she was swimming in the direction of the Old Landing. I wondered how she had survived since we last fed her more than a week ago. Ice covered the shallow water areas where she'd feed; there seemed to be little food available to sustain her. To me, the odds seemed stacked against her survival.

Slowly, Little One pushed her way toward us through the cold water strewn with small ice floes. The thin ice did not halt her; she resolutely pushed herself through it to reach our food. The adult swans were swimming on the other side of the docks, so for a while there was nothing to keep Little One from eating.

"Oh, Little One," I cried out. "You haven't had much to eat since we last fed you." How undernourished the little swan looked! She swallowed the bread so fast that we feared she would choke on it as it slipped down her neck. As quickly as she swallowed one piece, Little One searched for the next. My heart went out to her. Sam and

Samantha were just plain mean not to let such a small member of their species travel with them.

"Maybe Samantha is Little One's mother," I said.

"It's possible," Ralph answered. "If Little One is her offspring, Samantha would want her to leave," he continued. "However, Little One doesn't want to go." We had read that swan parents forced the spring cygnets to leave their birth site in the fall. It's the natural sequence, and then the parents will be ready to care for the new cygnets born the following spring.

Before Little One finished eating, the other two swans swam around the end of the wharf and discovered the little swan eating. Up went their wings as they increased their speed and charged toward Little One.

"Stop it!" I yelled at Sam.

My command went unheeded as both swans pursued the young bird. Little One hastily retreated through the icy slush, making her getaway. This did not stop the older swans; they veered to the right and continued to chase Little One. We watched the skirmish that continued until she reached Tabor's dock. Then the older swans broke off the chase. Sam swam over to Samantha, trumpeted and flexed his wings. In victory, Sam vigorously flapped his wings as his body rose perpendicular to the water. He looked like a football player waving his arms after delivering a tie-breaking touchdown.

"Let's go down to Tabor and see if Little One will come to eat there," Ralph suggested. "They will not let her come back here." As we left, Sam and Samantha swam northward up the center of the channel. Arriving at Tabor, we found that Little One had already passed the dock and was swimming southward.

"She's too far away to hear our calls," Ralph said. We drove to Island Wharf, arriving just before Little One rounded the harbormaster's dock.

Little One, seeing our food, quickly swam towards shore. Ralph tossed a few pieces of bread to her before offering a hand-held piece. Little One hungrily stretched her neck forward, hissed loudly at the out-stretched hand, then quickly gobbled the bread.

With the next piece, Ralph did not toss it so far out, trying to make Little One come closer to us. It worked! Little One ventured forward, with her wings raised and hissing loudly to appear big, bad, and ferocious. Quickly, her head darted forward and grabbed the bread.

Slowly, Ralph coaxed the swan into the shallow water. "She's so thin and scrawny," I cried out as she stood up to reach the food. Her emaciated body shocked us. Compared to the other two swans, she looked to be close to death's door. How could she possibly survive until spring without our help?

Ralph tossed the next piece of bread on the ground to see what Little One would do. Raising her wings higher, stretching her body to attain its fullest height and hissing still louder, she walked to the bread, and quickly ate it. Hissing, she looked at us and then searched the ground for more bread.

"I think she's had enough to eat," Ralph said when she had consumed three slices of bread. "We don't want her to become crop-bound." He remembered the flock of pigeons he raised as a child. "One pigeon didn't have the sense to stop eating when his crop was full. I'm not sure if swans can become crop-bound or not but let's not risk it. We can return later to give Little One more to eat."

We left Little One standing at the water edge, still looking for more food. "We'll be back. Stay here," I ordered the swan as though it could understand my command. "I hope the other two don't come down here and chase her away."

Returning a few hours later, we found Little One still near the town dock with her head underwater searching for food on her own. As her head came up for the second time, she heard our calls and swam to us. Already we represented food to her. Hungrily, she ate all the bread and still looked for more when we left.

Throughout the day, we returned three more times to feed her. Slowly, her hunger diminished. Luckily, Sam and Samantha stayed up around the Old Landing and Little One established her residency at Island Wharf, (the town dock).

From that day on, our feeding schedule was first to stop at the Old Landing to feed the older swans to keep them from wandering down to the town dock in search of food. Then we drove to Island Wharf to feed Little One. All three swans seem to know the plan and always waited in their assigned feeding places.

Chapter Ten

THE BATTLE

Through the rest of January and all of February, the swans stayed in their designated areas of the harbor. Occasionally, Little One wandered north to Tabor's dock. On one occasion when the other two swans saw Little One headed northward, they came charging down to evict her. Since it was mating season, Sam had no intentions of sharing his harbor with a third swan—big or little. Sam led the charge with his head tucked way back between his raised wings, fire in his eyes and ready to do battle. Samantha followed with her wings raised too. Little One knew, without a doubt, what the other two were telling her. She was in dangerous territory; she turned abruptly and swam southward back to the Island Wharf.

One delightful late winter afternoon, we left the house on a jaunt to capture the three swans on film. We found Little One feeding near Tabor and decided to coax her into the small marsh inlet to the south of the dock to feed her and take some pictures.

"The other two won't see us here," Ralph commented. "Little One can eat in peace." However, before the picture taking began, around the end of the dock swam Sam and Samantha!

"How did they know we were here?" I asked, puzzled by their sudden appearance.

"Sam must have recognized our car parked on the wharf and came looking for a snack."

However, Sam quickly forgot food when he saw who we were feeding. Seeing Sam, Little One quickly forgot all about food too. Sam came charging at the little swan. Little One was cornered. Her only escape was to slip through the opening under the dock, but to do so she had to swim towards Sam. She made a valiant effort and almost escaped, but as she came out the other side Sam was right behind her. Sam, seeming to sense victory at hand, increased his forward speed.

In panic, Little One moved to the left. This was a mistake, for that brought her up against the stone retaining wall. Sam continued the charge with his wings beating the water, making a loud smacking noise. Suddenly he brought his body half up out of the water and surged on top of Little One, pinning her against the wall. Next Sam grabbed the back of Little One's upper neck and forced her head underwater while continuing to thrash with his wings. Water splattered in every direction as Sam fought to keep Little One pinned down.

"Sam, Sam," I shouted, "Stop that!" I had visions of Little One floating lifeless when this encounter ended. "Do something," I begged Ralph.

Ralph was already climbing down the rocks towards the swans. Before he reached them, Little One managed to break away from Sam's hold. Without a backward glance, Little One darted toward the open harbor, swimming past Samantha who had watched the battle from a safe distance.

"Little One's okay," Ralph announced. "Did you notice how drenched and waterlogged she looked? The water has actually penetrated through her feathers. She's lucky that is all that happened to her. Sam is serving notice he doesn't want her in his harbor!"

Little One slipped around the end of the dock, and retreated from the battlefield. One very soggy cygnet departed in defeat. Turning back to scold Sam, I saw that he had not come through the battle unscathed.

"Sam's injured," I called out in alarm. A small patch of blood glistened on his wing.

"He scraped his wing on the stones while he was thrashing Little One," Ralph explained. "It's not broken. It looks like it has already stopped bleeding."

As Sam began to preen the feathers around the injury, Samantha swam over to him. Peace returned to the area. What had been a noisy thrashing arena a few minutes ago was now tranquil; only Sam's wing gave evidence of what had taken place.

"Sam can be a formidable enemy when he's angry," Ralph stated. "I'd hate to be in the water with him when he's provoked."

The event triggered a memory of something that happened last summer. One afternoon as we fed Sam at the boat ramp, a woman we knew stood and watched us.

"Come closer if you want," Ralph said. "You won't frighten Sam."

"Not on your life," she answered emphatically. "I think you are crazy to get so close to that swan."

Her attitude surprised us. "He won't bother you," I reassured her.

"I'm not so sure about that!" she answered. "Two years ago I was sitting in our skiff, relaxing and reading. I closed my eyes to rest them. The next thing I felt was a thud against the side of the boat. When I opened my eyes, Sam's long neck was reaching over the side of the boat. Before I knew what was happening, Sam nipped my toe. He was trying to get in the boat," she continued. "I had to use my oar to make him back off. I'll never get close to that swan."

After watching Sam's attack on Little One, I finally understood how frightened the woman must have been. Our special friend had a hostile side to his personality that we had not seen before. It had been hard for us to accept the stories of Sam's anger as true until today.

After the battle between Sam and Little One, we fed Little One at the Island Wharf only. We did not want any harm to come to our smallest friend.

Little One's white feathers and buff colored feet puzzled us. We read that cygnets are born with brown down and their feathers remain the same color until the following year. We knew by the absence of a black knob that Little One was almost a year old. Incorrectly, we assumed all young cygnets had light-colored feet. At the library Ralph discovered the real reason for Little One's white feathers and pale feet: she was a Polish mute swan.

As the days lengthened, the older swans roamed about the open harbor. Occasionally when they saw Little One, Sam would chase her. However, the big battle never repeated. Little One managed to stay out of their way for the most part.

The real reason for Little One's white feathers and pale feet:
she was a Polish mute swan.

Chapter Eleven

A LOVE SCORNED

Arriving at the Old Landing one March afternoon, we did not find the swans waiting for us. The brisk east wind whipped the water into a mosaic of green-gray waves, each capped with what looked like softly beaten egg-white foam. The low, gray clouds paraded without regimental precision across the overcast sky. We scanned the harbor, searching for the missing birds.

"Look in the sky over Ram Island," I suggested to Ralph as I looked through the binoculars and saw two swans gaining altitude over the southern end of the harbor. Next, the swans flew to the right towards Silvershell Beach and soon were out of sight. Did Sam have more visitors in his harbor?

"But I don't see Sam," I continued searching the harbor with the binoculars hoping to locate the swan riding the whitecaps.

"Let's go to Silvershell to see if the other two landed there," Ralph suggested. "On our way, we can look for Sam."

"I see him," Ralph said as we drove along Water Street. "He's to the north of Nye's wharf, paddling at top speed as though he has a destination in mind. He must have seen the other two swans fly towards Silvershell and he's heading there the only way he can." Poor Sam! It must be terrible for him to flap his wings and not be able to get airborne, especially when he wants to fly with other swans."

"Look at what's going on," an astonished Ralph said when we arrived at Silvershell. Samantha and Little One were swimming peacefully together. This was not what we expected. As we watched, Samantha approached Little One and nodded her head, a gesture for friendship among swans.

"You're fraternizing with the enemy," I scolded Samantha. She was definitely not being loyal to her Sam! Little One, confused by the older swan's overtures of friendship, tentatively retreated. However, when Samantha didn't attack, Little One went back to eating.

79

"Here comes Sam," Ralph announced a few minutes later as a very determined Sam swam around the spit of land separating the inner and outer harbor. Steadily, he swam across the water between Nye's wharf and the breakwater at the south end of Silvershell Beach.

"Sam, Sam," we called to him. However, he did not acknowledge our presence.

Once around the breakwater, he appeared angry at what he saw. Quickly, he raised his wings, folded his long neck back between them, and placed his head on the underside of his lowered neck. His increased speed created a wake as he propelled himself forward to evict Little One, the intruder, and to protect Samantha.

What happened next surprised Sam and us. Sensing the danger of a very irate swan coming towards her, Little One walked up the bank to the safety of dry land.

Samantha was not intimidated; she charged at Sam. Startled by her reaction, Sam's assault halted at once. He made a hundred and eighty degree turn to escape from the advancing Samantha. With her powerful wings fully extended, Samantha menacingly slapped the water surface as she chased Sam. She continued the chase until he disappeared around the end of the breakwater.

Once on the other side, Sam discovered the chase had ended. As we watched, Sam swam back around to the south side of the breakwater as though he did not believe what had happened. He approached Samantha and Little One with his wings still raised. Again, Samantha chased him. This definitely was more than a lover's quarrel. Again, Sam retreated to the north side of the breakwater. For a third time, he swam around the breakwater. Samantha was busy eating. This time he approached her with his wings down. Sam nodded his head several times as he came closer to her and spoke in his soft purr voice. Samantha neither chased him nor returned the soft murmurs or gave any signs of recognition. Only dead silence answered Sam's attempts at reconciliation.

"Sam's being rejected as a mate." Ralph gave words to our thoughts. "She's ignoring him!"

"Oh, Sam," I cried out as my heart ached for him. At that moment our feelings toward Samantha were not loving.

Sam, too, understood what had happened, for he swam away. The dejected flightless swan swam swiftly back to the inner harbor with his head high. Our hearts ached for him but he was alone on the water and out of our reach.

"Let's see if we can coax him in at the town wharf," Ralph suggested. "He needs comforting." However, he did not respond to our calls from the wharf. "He's swimming straight down the center of the harbor."

Finally at the Old Landing boat ramp, his 'at home' place, Sam came ashore. Seeing us waiting for him, his forward speed did not lessen as he reached shallow water. Quickly getting up on his feet, he charged up the beach to me. Sam grabbed my pant leg and held on as I caressed his head, neck, and back.

"It's all right, Sam. We love you and always will," I spoke firmly but softly. My words were only sounds to Sam. It was just as impossible for him to comprehend their meaning as it was for me to understand his mute swan language. However, I hoped he sensed the level of loving concern in my voice.

"Sam, corn bread," coaxed Ralph as he set the food dish in front of him. However, Sam showed no interest in food and kept his tight hold on my pant leg.

"Its okay, Sam, everything will be all right in a short space of time. The world will keep spinning on its axis as it must. Rejection is as hard for a swan as it is for a human," comforted Ralph as I continued to caress our jilted swan.

I felt as though a child of mine was rejected. I was ready and willing to chase both Samantha and Little One away from Sippican Harbor. This was Sam's home and if the other two swans did not want to be friends with him then they should leave. In the gathering dusk, the inner harbor area felt empty and cold where only twenty-four hours ago it had a feeling of fullness and warmth.

"It's getting dark, we must let Sam settle down for the night," Ralph said after the swan ate some food. "Time to go."

Our hearts ached at the thought of him being alone under the stars. Sadly, we left Sam standing on the darkening beach. His white feathers vividly reflected the last faint glow of daylight as night took reign.

After a ten-week relationship, Samantha had rejected the flightless Sam as a possible mate. It is a rigid law of nature that survival belongs to the fittest. We assumed that a swan with a broken wing did not measure up as a good mate. That was the only explanation that made sense. "Let's go see how Sam is doing," Ralph suggested after supper. "He's probably sleeping on his favorite rock in the inlet near Daggett House."

"Sam, why aren't you sleeping?" a surprised Ralph asked when we found him still floating in the water at the boat ramp. Sam, recognizing us, gave a head nod and wiggled his tail.

As I walked down the beach, Sam came ashore in the dark and I comforted him again. This time when we offered Sam food by car light, he ate heartily.

"Are you feeling better, Sam?" Ralph asked. We assumed so; for with his hunger satisfied, he returned to the water.

"He's beginning to recover from Samantha's rejection." We watched him leave until he became a ghostly shadow in the distance and finally disappeared. We went home feeling somewhat better after seeing our friend a second time.

"Do you think Samantha and Little One will now try to chase Sam from the harbor?" I asked later that evening.

"I don't think Sam will be easily evicted from his home. There could be a turf battle for awhile but I think Sam will prevail. Remember how he trounced Little One not too long ago."

I worried all night and wondered what we could do to assist Sam in this territorial battle.

The next morning, we arrived at the Old Landing before seven o'clock. I expected Samantha to appear at the usual breakfast time, possibly with Little One tagging along. We intended to be there to support Sam in his battle for his home territory, although we had no inkling of what we could do to help. Our concerns for Sam grew when he wasn't waiting for breakfast. I had visions of the other two swans forcing Sam from the harbor.

At the town dock, I found out how wrong I was. It was Sam who was doing the evicting. In full battle position, Sam charged at Samantha and Little One, chasing them southward out of his harbor. Sam had the situation under control.

As we watched, it became apparent to us that he was chasing Samantha. Little One was chased only because she was there.

"It's just as I told you last night; Sam is not going to be evicted from his home. He's giving Samantha her walking papers," Ralph said.

There was no doubt that Sam was still boss bird in Sippican Harbor and very capable of making that fact known to other swans.

When Sam successfully chased the two beyond Nye's wharf, he began to swim back towards the town dock. Samantha, because she wasn't being chased, turned around and began to re-enter the inner harbor again. Little One fell in behind her, tagging along like a lonely puppy.

When Sam came abreast of the town dock, he noticed Samantha was following some distance behind him. He promptly turned about, and again the chase was on with Samantha the target. This time, Sam chased the two to the south of Nye's wharf before returning to the inner harbor. Four times the skirmish repeated itself as a very determined Sam chased Samantha from the inner harbor.

"Do you suppose Samantha regrets her actions of last night and wants to be friends with Sam?" I wondered.

"If that's the case, Sam's not interested in reconciliation. He is not willing to forgive and forget," Ralph answered. "We might as well go home. Until he gets Samantha to stay out of the inner harbor, he will not come to eat." I was elated that Sam was in control of his harbor.

"Its okay, Sam, everything will be all right in a short space of time."

Chapter Twelve

ANOTHER SWAN

As the days passed, Samantha and Little One continued to try to move back into the inner harbor. But Sam was just as determined to keep them out. A cat and mouse game occurred daily among the swans. If they wandered too far into the harbor, Sam firmly set about chasing them back to Nye's wharf. It seemed very unlikely to us that the three swans would ever live together peacefully in Sippican Harbor.

"Look at what's going on," Ralph exclaimed when we arrived at the Old Landing a week after Samantha's rejection. To our surprise, the three swans were feeding together off Black Point.

Sam, answering the blinking of our car lights, swam to the ramp. Samantha, seeing him swimming towards us, followed. Not wanting to be left behind, Little One tagged along, keeping some distance between the older swans and her.

"Are you all friends again?" I asked my favorite swan, as he walked to his dish. A minute later Samantha arrived at the water edge and stood up. Immediately, Sam turned about and faced her. His head hung low, his wings rose; he marched toward her with a definite 'you're not welcome here' posture.

"Samantha knows what Sam's action is conveying," Ralph said. Choosing retreat, she quietly turned, slipped into a swimming position. Holding her long neck straight as an arrow, she turned her head and kept an eye on an aggressive Sam as she swam away.

Satisfied with Samantha's decision, Sam returned to eating. Several minutes later, Samantha again tried to walk up the beach. "Sam, finish your meal," I ordered when he turned to drive her off. "I won't let her eat your bread."

Seeing Sam's aggressive stance, Samantha again returned to the water and swam away. Beyond her, Little One floated peacefully.

Witnessing the power play between the other two, the little swan wisely chose not to join in the conflict.

"Sam's not about to share his food," Ralph said. "Samantha wants to eat from the dish they've always shared. Sam's memory is good; it appears he hasn't forgotten what happened a week ago. She can swim with him but that's all."

Finishing his meal, Sam entered the water. Although he did not chase her, Samantha retreated farther out as he swam away. "There definitely is a change in the pecking order between the adult swans."

We wondered what had caused Samantha's change in attitude toward Sam. Was it hunger or a desire to be with her former companion?

As Sam disappeared around the end of the wharf, Samantha headed to the beach. "Let's give her some food," Ralph suggested. "She won't understand why we are not feeding her. If Sam comes back, we'll stop. I suspect that when she sees him approaching; she will forget about food."

While Samantha walked to the dish, Little One slowly swam towards shore. As she got closer to the beach, Samantha raised her wings in warning. The little swan stopped immediately. In the natural hierarchy of mutes, Little One was a low swan in *Cygnus Olor* hierarchy and acted accordingly.

Finally, with her hunger satisfied, Samantha returned to the water but made no attempt to chase the younger swan as she swam back to Black Point. "It's your turn, Little One," Ralph called out as he refilled the empty dish. Without much fanfare Little One ate and went on her way, following Samantha towards Black Point. "Let's hope Sam lets the others eat with him before long. It takes more than an hour to feed each one separately."

Soon, as though in answer to our wishes, the swans became a three-some, swimming and eating together. Where you saw one, the other two were close by. We were surprised to see a closer relationship developing between Sam and Little One. We delighted in the thought of having not one swan friend but three!

At a morning feeding three weeks later, only Sam was waiting at the Old Landing. "Well Sam, has there been another dispute between you and the other swans? Did you chase them off again?" I questioned.

"What do you think happened between them?" I asked Ralph. "They were getting along so splendidly I was sure they would stay together."

"It's hard to say. They're probably down near Tabor or Island Wharf. We'll check there when Sam finishes."

We searched in vain, even checking the marsh at Silvershell thinking they might have gone there. They had vanished! I wondered if Sam decided they had to leave, or was it their choice? As usual, my question went unanswered.

Once again, we settled into the routine of feeding one swan. Mealtime was less hectic and we renewed our close friendship with Sam. It had been hard to have a one-on-one relationship with Sam while Samantha and Little One were present. When the other swans were there, he appeared not to want much stroking or interplay with us. Now Sam insisted on playing with Ralph at the end of his meals. Suddenly we realized how much we had missed those special times with our favorite swan.

Then one May afternoon Sam's life changed once again. Half way through the meal, we heard the rhythmic sound of swan wings in flight, quickly followed by the splash of water as a pair of swans landed just beyond the Knowlton House breakwater. Sam heard it also. He abruptly stopped eating and entered the water with his wings high. He knew where they had landed and quickly swam to an opening in the outer end of the breakwater and disappeared.

"They're back," I shouted joyfully. "Samantha and Little One have returned!"

"Wouldn't that be something?" Ralph answered. "One swan appeared to be dirty. Where do you suppose they've been to get so grubby?"

From the breakwater, we watched as the two swans swam toward Tabor with Sam in hot pursuit. Picking up the feeding dish, we drove to Tabor's dock to see what was happening with the swans.

"Darn, Sam's still chasing them," Ralph said. "Let's go to Island Wharf beach. Maybe they'll stop there. They won't be back this way."

However, we did not find the new arrivals there. Looking northward, we saw Sam was headed back to the Old Landing. Had Sam chased them away?

"They're somewhere between here and Tabor," Ralph said, breaking into my thoughts. "I really thought we would find them here where we fed Little One most of the winter. Maybe they slipped into the marshy inlet behind the bandstand."

From the stone wall behind the bandstand, we saw the swans feeding in the inlet behind one of Tabor's dormitories. "I'm sure no one will object to our driving down the dirt road to reach the swans."

"Little One," Ralph called as we walked down the beach. There was no doubt one swan was our young winter friend. However, the second one was not Samantha.

"Who's your friend?" Ralph asked Little One as she walked up the beach to her dish. It was a young swan, still showing some adolescent brown feathers on its body. These gave it a drab and dirty look, in sharp contrast to the beautiful white feathers that Little One wore.

Little One ate while the new arrival watched from a distance. Whenever I made a move toward her, she backed away.

We quietly continued feeding Little One. I tossed bread out to the floating swan. At first, she acted as though she had no idea what to do with it. Finally, she tentatively tried a piece that landed in front of her. She ate a few more pieces before Little One joined her in the water. Slowly, they glided back to the inlet. There, she began eating her natural food, the sea grasses.

"Stay down here out of Sam's sight," I instructed Little One as dusk began to settle and it was time for us to go.

Back home, we wondered if Little One had returned to Sippican Harbor because she had chosen it as her permanent home. Where was Samantha? Where had Little One found this new friend? Again we had more questions than answers that night.

The next morning, Sam was waiting for us at the Old Landing. As he ate, we scanned the harbor looking for the missing swans. They were nowhere in sight. When Sam swam off towards the beach at Black Point after eating, we began a search for Little One and her new friend.

At Tabor, we found a few Canada geese feeding. Next, we stopped at the beach where we had fed them the previous night. There they were, eating breakfast in the quiet inlet.

"Little One," Ralph called out and the swan came to eat. The new swan cautiously swam toward us but stayed a short distance from shore.

"Toss some bread closer to shore," Ralph suggested. "Maybe you can coax her to come closer."

Reluctant to move nearer to us, she did eat the tossed bread by stretching her long neck as far as possible. I studied her as she ate. She was probably two years old, no more than that since most of the feathers hidden by her folded wings were a soft dappled brown. White feathers covered the rest of her body, with a sprinkling of brown ones. Her head was symmetrical with a small black knob protruding over a reddish-pink smooth bill—definitely a young pen (female mute swan).

"She's intently watching what Little One is doing," Ralph broke into my thoughts. "But she's not ready to join Little One on the beach."

"Do you suppose she has known other humans?"

"I think so. Otherwise, she wouldn't be this close to us. Have you noticed she hasn't made a sound yet?"

"You're right!" I answered unable to recall ever hearing a peep from her. "She hasn't even communicated with Little One since she arrived. Do you suppose she's really a *mute* mute swan?"

"She probably doesn't have much to say," Ralph rejoined. As was customary, Little One returned to the water once she finished eating. Unlike Sam, she had not developed a desire to play with Ralph at the end of her meal.

Over the course of the next week, Sam ate at the Old Landing while the others ate at the boathouse beach. A few days later, Sam discovered us feeding the two swans in the almost hidden inlet. He quickly made his displeasure known by chasing them south of Island Wharf. Evidently, Sam laid claim to the harbor north of Island Wharf and did not tolerate any visitors. However, we did manage to feed all three swans daily.

"Its time to give her a name," Ralph said. "Any suggestions?"

"I like Missy. It's an appropriate name – she's young and female."

"Then Missy she'll be."

In the days that followed, Missy began to walk up on the beach when Little One ate. She always stayed a few yards away. Little One expressed her growing trust in us by sitting down beside Ralph as she ate. Sometimes, after eating, she stayed there and preened her feathers.

"Can I help?" Ralph asked one afternoon as Little One began to fluff up her feathers. Gently, Ralph reached over and stroked the swan's chest feathers.

"Cronk," Little One squawked her protest. When Ralph continued to touch her, Little One latched on to his shirtsleeve. There was no fear in her reaction to being touched.

"You have been accepted by Little One," I said, watching Ralph gently scratch the swan's chin. All the while, Missy was quietly watching the interplay. I would have loved to be able to read her mind at that moment!

A few days later, Missy approached us as we played with Little One on the beach. Silently, without moving an inch, we held our breaths as she came up to us. Giving us the once over, she lowered her head into the corn dish and began to slurp noisily.

"Wow," I said in a whisper.

"Missy, do you like cracked corn?" inquired Ralph. As if to answer his question, Missy ate more corn. Missy towered over us as we sat on

the sand. When she raised her head to swallow, I marveled at the graceful line of her body, the gentle curve of her long neck that traveled down over her chest, the elliptical sag of her tummy that continued upward to the end of her tail feathers. A pair of short black legs supported that sleek sturdy body. She was destined to be a magnificent pen!

Too quickly, the moment passed and Missy walked back into the water. Little One followed. Still awed by the experience, we sat quietly on the beach watching the swans.

"Wasn't that something?" Ralph mused. "To have her stand so close to us and calmly eat."

"Her trust in us is growing."

"Have you noticed," Ralph asked, "with each new swan we meet, it takes less time for them to trust us than it did with Sam? It was six months before Sam would approach us on land. With Samantha and Little One it took only a few weeks. Missy has only taken ten days to come to us on the beach."

"She should have her own feeding dish," I commented.

Once Missy began to come up on the beach to eat, the bond between us grew rapidly. In a matter of days, she also sat on the sand beside us to preen. To our utter surprise, one morning she completed her preening, tucked her bill under her wing and went to sleep. Every so often, an eye popped open to check on the activity going on around her but her head stayed down.

"Can I touch?" Ralph asked Missy one morning as we all sat on the small beach enjoying the spring sunshine. Slowly, he reached out and gently stroked Missy's chest. Quickly she got to her feet and stared down at the hand that had touched her.

"It's okay, Missy," Ralph spoke softly to her. As she looked at him, he slowly stroked her feathers. Missy's eyes followed the movement of the hand touching her. Next, she reached for Ralph's shirtsleeve and latched on to it. The wings started to rise, but quickly folded back into place as she accepted Ralph's touch. Another milestone was attained.

The following days brought closer and closer contact with Missy. First, a gentle touch on the chest, next a chin scratch, followed by a tummy rub. Soon, the more Ralph stroked Missy's tummy the closer she tried to get. This definitely was a swan that loved tummy rubs.

Before long, the two swans began wandering northward in the direction of the Old Landing. For a while, Sam chased them away. However, persistence won out and soon the three swans were together. Life among the swans was as serene as the harbor water on a calm morning.

Our joy that spring knew no bounds; three swans to love and play with. Just when we felt life with three swans would go on forever, Little One and Missy left. Whereas before our joy had soared to great heights, now our sadness sunk in a deep and bottomless pit. The hardest thing to fathom was why they left.

Sam adjusted quickly to being a lone swan once more. At each feeding at the Old Landing, we listened for the rhythmic sound of swan wings overhead, announcing the return of Little One and Missy. As the days passed, our hopes dimmed.

Soon, the more Ralph stroked Missy's tummy the closer she tried to get. This definitely was a swan that loved tummy rubs.

Chapter Thirteen

A TRIP TO THE DOCTOR

Life with only one swan settled into a routine schedule of two meals a day. Frequently, Ralph stopped at the Old Landing at noon to see if Sam was around. With an almost empty harbor to roam in, Sam often was off on a personal inspection tour of his harbor. At feeding time, if he was not waiting for us at the Old Landing, we sighted him swimming down the middle of the harbor, coming for his meal. He sometimes tarried along the way to nibble the algae on winter mooring sticks.

Arriving at the Old Landing one early May evening, we found Sam lying on the western bank of Black Point. We signaled to him by blinking the car lights and blowing the horn. He made no effort to come for supper.

"He's looking this way," Ralph commented, "he knows we are here." We watched Sam twitch first one wing and then the other, in rhythmic movement.

"Sam's hurt!" I observed looking through the binoculars. "There's bright red blood covering the wing tips and most of his tail. Here, take a look."

"Looks like he's been bleeding for awhile," Ralph exclaimed. "We've got to reach him quickly." He already had the car in motion. "We'll stop at home to get something to carry him in; he may need medical care. Even if the injury isn't bleeding, we can't leave him on Black Point, he's not safe lying there all night."

"I'll grab a sheet; we don't have a box large enough to hold him."

In an unbelievably short span of time, we got the sheet and secured permission to walk across the private property to reach Sam. We crossed the marsh in record time.

Not wanting to frighten the swan, we stopped when we were within twenty feet of him. "Hello Sam," I called softly to reassure the swan it was friends approaching. Sam, facing us, intently watched our progress.

95

"See if you can get closer to him," Ralph suggested. "If he heads toward the water, I'll block his way." Once Sam entered the water, it would be impossible to capture him.

I approached the swan with a piece of cornbread in my hand. He did not try to stand. The only sign of his concern was the slight raising of his wings. I continued talking to him while Ralph joined us.

It was a shock to see so much blood covering his white feathers. We made a quick visual search of his body to locate the wound but did not find it.

"Get him to stand," Ralph suggested. "Maybe the cut is on his leg."

When I held my hand up to offer him cornbread, Sam stood up to reach it but still Ralph did not find the wound. As I took a step back from Sam, he moved towards me.

"There's a cut on the bottom of his right foot," Ralph said. "As he steps forward, he leaves a blotch of blood on the ground. Hold the bread up higher. See if he'll stretch upward to reach it."

Sam did stretch to reach the cornbread. He put his weight on the front of his right foot and raised the heel off the ground. "I see it!" Ralph said. "There's a cut on the heel of his right foot."

"Is it bleeding a lot?" I asked.

"I can see the blood spurt out of the wound. We need to take him to the vet."

As I talked to Sam, Ralph gently slipped the sheet over Sam's head, around his body and under the webbed feet, being careful not to cause further harm to the oozing cut. Surprisingly, Sam never struggled to get away.

"Want me to help carry him?" I offered.

"Let's see if I can do it myself. If we each carry an end of the sheet, his weight will be resting on the injured foot. It'll be better for Sam if I can carry him myself. You can help if my arms give out."

Across the field we headed, Ralph gently carrying the injured swan. Three quarters of the way to the car, Ralph's right arm weakened. Coming up beside him, I propped up the arm supporting Sam's body weight with my hand. I was shocked to see that blood had seeped through the sheet and covered Ralph's clothes. So much blood covered Sam, the sheet and Ralph. How much blood could Sam lose before it would endanger his life?

As we hastened on our way, we silently prayed this was a night the animal hospital was open. Reaching the car, I quickly opened the tailgate of the station wagon and climbed in. Ralph gently placed the injured swan beside me. I peeked under the sheet to see how Sam was doing. His bill was resting on his chest, and a dejected eye stared at me. I reached under the sheet and stroked his chest. Sam did not move. Silently, without a sharp honk of protest, he endured his predicament.

Arriving at the Marion Animal Hospital, we found cars in the parking lot and the lights on inside. Ralph went in to see when the vet could see the swan. A few minutes later, he was carrying Sam into the brightly-lit examining room.

Dr. Tremblay immediately diagnosed the extent of Sam's injury. The swan had sustained a cut, perhaps from stepping on a piece of broken glass. Although the wound was small, it was deep. However, to our great relief, the vet said Sam would recover. While he performed the needed medical services, I lovingly stroked the still sheet-covered Sam and told him it was going to hurt for a moment or two.

I remembered comforting our small children years ago when an injury caused a quick trip to the pediatrician's office. I wondered if Sam received any comfort upon hearing my voice. All during the procedure he lay quietly on the cold hard examining table, only shaking his injured foot when the doctor cauterized the wound. A quick dab of ointment completed the procedure. Dr. Tremblay advised us to keep Sam's injured foot dry overnight if possible.

"No problem," we said. "We'll keep him at home for the night." Where in the house does one keep an injured thirty-pound swan? The cellar was the logical place but it was unacceptable to us. The new laundry room was the appropriate place for such an honored guest.

"You stay with Sam," Ralph suggested when we arrived home. "I'll empty the laundry room and spread papers on the floor."

"Be sure to remove the small items on the lower shelves."

"Don't worry. I'll take care of everything. Just keep Sam quiet. If he thrashes about, he might reopen the wound." Noticing Sam's head poking out from under the sheet Ralph asked, "Should we cover him up again?"

"No, he'll be all right." I answered as Sam calmly looked out the car windows as if it was something he did every day.

Before I knew it, Ralph was opening the tailgate. Again, we draped the sheet over Sam's head to keep him from becoming alarmed. I ran up the stairs and opened the door. As the door chimes rang, I wondered what Sam thought of that strange sound.

Ralph placed the swan on the laundry room floor and for the second time that evening, Sam found himself in new surroundings. First his head turned in one direction and then the other. Soon he tilted his head to the side, eyeing the things on the upper shelves. Sam calmly accepted this new location.

To make Sam feel at ease Ralph placed his dish in front of him. Quickly, I added the water and cracked corn. However, the favored cornbread seemed to reassure Sam he was among friends, although in an unfamiliar place. He certainly was a pathetic looking swan with all that blood on his feathers. Sam faced a major cleanup task once he returned to the harbor. I knew how meticulous he was in keeping himself clean but I doubted that Sam could ever clean those bloodstained feathers to glistening white again.

In the past, when the winter weather was at its worst, Ralph and I often wished our special swan could be snug at home with us instead of sleeping on the windswept ice. Having Sam as a houseguest was a dream come true.

Many times during the evening one of us walked down the hallway, now cluttered with laundry room items, to check on Sam. We found him sitting down, intently looking to see who or what was opening the creaking door. Whenever either of us entered the kitchen making noises that would seem strange to Sam, we called out 'Good Morning, Sam' to reassure him.

Our cat Holly, planning to use the litter box, got the surprise of his life when he poked his head through the small swinging door he used to enter the laundry room. Quickly, he backed away and bumped into the boxes on the floor behind him. His eyes were as round as silver dollars and his presence silently stated, 'What was that? Maybe I don't need to use the litter box after all,' and promptly relieved himself on the carpet.

The next morning there was no evidence of blood seeping from Sam's wound; it was time to return him to the harbor. "We'll feed him first," Ralph said. "We know from our Hurricane Gloria experience that once he sees the water, food will be the last thing on his mind."

Sadly, I prepared Sam's breakfast. Our honored guest had to leave. I knew, deep down, that Sam belonged in the harbor with the bright blue sky above and the warm sun shining on him. However, I have never been very good at saying goodbye to people, and now I was heavy-hearted over Sam's approaching departure.

It was when Ralph backed the car up to the boat ramp at the Old Landing that Sam knew he was home. He repeatedly bumped his bill against the back window, trying to reach the water.

Ralph opened the tailgate, picked up Sam and started to carry him down the beach. The closer Sam got to the water, the more he looked like a canine pointer with his long neck pointing straight to the water.

Soon the large black feet were walking through the air as they escaped the retaining sheet.

Ralph placed Sam on the beach at the water's edge and removed the sheet. Without a backward glance, he entered the water and swam towards the middle of the inner harbor. A hundred feet from shore he fastidiously began bathing, obviously happy to be back where he belonged.

It was time to return Sam to the harbor

"That injured leg is bothering Sam," Ralph said five days later. Sam seemed to be favoring it. Most of the time, he held it up out of the water, resting it straight back over his tail. We had seen him do that many times in the past. In fact, it is quite common to see swans slowly gliding on the water with a foot resting fully extended over their tail. However, when Sam tried to stand on the injured foot, he quickly took his weight off it, suggesting he felt pain. Although the wound had healed, the injured leg appeared swollen.

"I'll visit the vet again," I decided, "and see what he advises."

Dr. Tremblay gave me ten tetracycline capsules with the instructions to give Sam one capsule morning and night, but he did not tell me how I was to accomplish this feat. Whenever one of our cats needed medication, I gently held the cat between my knees, opened its mouth, and placed the capsule on the back of the tongue. Then I stroked the cat's neck to make her swallow the pill. I knew this would not work with Sam. If I was to get the medication into Sam, I must use the favored cornbread as the route. Ralph suggested placing the whole capsule in a piece of cornbread.

"It won't work. Once Sam feels the capsule in his mouth he'll spit it out," I said, remembering how quickly Sam would eject a piece of unwanted food from his mouth. "I know; we can spike his cornbread with the medication," I suggested. "I can use a drinking straw to drill a small hole in the middle of a small piece of cornbread. I'll pour the contents from one capsule into the hole, and then gently tap the piece to settle the powder. Then I'll use the cornbread from the straw as a plug to keep the medication in place."

"That seems feasible."

"What if he senses something different about the spiked cornbread?" I asked.

"Give Sam a couple of pieces of unadulterated cornbread before offering him a spiked piece," Ralph suggested. "He'll eat it so fast he won't have time to taste it."

"I'll fix a couple of pieces of the spiked cornbread. There's a good chance that the first piece may crumble in the feeding dish before it's eaten."

At the Old Landing, we found Sam across the water lying on a favorite grassy bank. Although we signaled to him, Sam did not make any effort to come. "His foot must be too painful to use," I commented. "We'll have to feed him over there tonight."

Since I was the one who usually fed Sam, we decided I should approach him alone. Ralph drove me to where I could walk the eastern shore to reach Sam. He then returned to the Old Landing to observe the impending procedure through the binoculars.

Entering the open marsh, I called to Sam, wanting him to know he had nothing to fear. Sam watched my progress without getting up on his feet. I decided to approach Sam from the water-side, cutting off his escape route. I walked cautiously and slowly towards the injured swan. Sam showed no signs of fear or panic. From this, I assumed Sam's foot was too painful to support his weight. As I got closer, I crouched down so my height would not threaten him.

Reaching the swan, I set the familiar feeding dish with its polystyrene collar down on the grass in front of him, quickly adding the cracked corn, water, and some cornbread. Without hesitation Sam ate, gulping down the two pieces of unadulterated cornbread. With a silent prayer, I offered Sam the spiked cornbread. Quickly, Sam took it into his bill and swallowed. I observed its progress down his long neck, watching the movement of the lump that marked its location on the inside. Slowly it rippled downward. Sam had not noticed anything different about that piece of cornbread. I quickly fed him two more pieces of 'normal' cornbread. Sam had taken his first dose of the antibiotic. One down, only nine more to go, I noted silently.

When Sam finished eating and the gnats decided to have me for their evening meal, I decided to leave. I realized Sam had not stood during the feeding; another sure sign the injured foot had infection festering within.

As I gathered the feeding dish and food, Sam lay quietly and watched. Slowly, I backed away from him on my hands and knees, sliding the food supplies noiselessly over the grass. When I was twenty feet away from him, I slowly rose to my feet as I continued to talk to the swan. Sam did not move an inch. With a final goodbye to Sam I continued on my way.

Back home, Ralph and I worried about Sam's safety there on the marsh grass. The injury put him at a disadvantage. However, we had done all we could. Now we had to let go and trust in something beyond ourselves to keep him safe during the night. I thought it was like parenting; there comes a time when you must let your child go beyond your safe, loving reach. We reassured ourselves that Sam did know how to take care of himself.

The next morning we joyfully saw Sam swimming. He came to the water's edge at the boat ramp to eat. I gave him two normal pieces of cornbread before I fed him the medicated one. The second dose of medication was administered successfully. Although Sam would not stand on the injured foot yet, we knew he'd recover completely in a few days.

During this time, I fed Sam by myself until he had taken the medication, and then Ralph joined us on the beach.

A short five days later, Sam was almost back to normal. Again the foot propelled him swiftly through the water and supported his hefty body as he stood to preen and oil his feathers.

Since that medical emergency, we have said many prayers of thanks for Dr. Tremblay's medical care. Once again, our feathered friend swam proudly about his harbor home.

Chapter Fourteen

ANOTHER SURPRISE

Fully recovered, Sam now began attacking the boats launched at the Old Landing. Although he did not have a pen sitting on eggs, Sam was fiercely territorial during the spring mating season. It seemed as though Sam considered the harbor belonged to him and the boats were intruders. Thus, he valiantly protected his turf in the only way he could, regardless of the size of the boat. If he had use of his wings, he would have been a potential terror. By late June, Sam abruptly stopped harassing the boats. Without another swan to share his days and nights, he reverted to his bachelor ways of snoozing on the marsh whenever he felt like it.

Ralph and I were busy learning the rules of boating. The previous November we had purchased a twenty-seven foot cabin cruiser. Our sudden involvement in boating began very innocently and grew rapidly.

"If we had a pair of oars," Ralph remarked one day the previous June, "we could use the old skiff to find out where Sam goes during the day."

Two weeks later, guess what he got for Father's Day—a new pair of oars. By July 4, we owned a 5 Hp. outboard engine. After a few of months of cruising among the big boats moored in Sippican Harbor, we succumbed to a very common illness that strikes all boat owners: the desire for a larger boat. We researched the pros and cons of different makes of boats. By late November of that year, we owned a 1984 Albin 27. Ours was the only boat cruising Sippican Harbor in early December 1985! We had demonstrated to our friends and neighbors the lengths to which we would go to observe the swans.

Selecting a name for our new boat proved to be difficult; with each suggestion quickly voted down. "I have the perfect name," Ralph declared while at the library one afternoon. "Cygnus Olor. What do you think?"

"How'd you come up with that name?"

"It's the scientific name for mute swan," Ralph answered. "It describes our boat—big and white."

"Very clever!" I admitted. It was a classy name. Our obsession with swans was now apparent to everyone. The following spring Cygnus Olor joined Puffin, Sea Lark, Sea Owl and Shearwater moored in Sippican Harbor.

"Look across," Ralph said as we arrived at the Old Landing on the last day of June. There in Sam's lagoon, two swans were swimming together.

"Little One is back," I shouted. She was the only swan we knew that left Sippican Harbor and returned.

"Sam knows the newest arrival," Ralph replied. "But from this distance, it's hard to tell if it's Little One."

"We don't have enough food for two swans. You watch them and I'll go home for the other dish and more food."

Upon my return, we signaled to Sam by flashing the car lights. He responded quickly.

"It must be Little One," I commented, as the second swan followed Sam.

"Missy!" Ralph called out in surprise. There was no doubt. Without hesitation, she walked up the beach to greet us.

Soon the two swans were eating side by side as though Missy had never left. How delightful it was that she returned. Sam's acquiescence to Missy's presence seemed to express his contentment to have her back.

Where was Little One? Why hadn't she returned with Missy? Did Missy's return mean she was choosing Sam for a mate? How we wished we could communicate with her!

In the following weeks, feeding visits became pleasurable events as Missy's relationship with us deepened. At first, Missy gently nibbled at my hand as I stretched it out toward her. Then she allowed me to rub her chin as she held onto my coat sleeve. Several days later, she consented to having me stroke her long neck. Soon, Missy was coming closer and closer to me during our feeding visits.

"Missy, you are a beautiful bird," I said as I caressed her from chin to tummy. Quickly, her head dipped down and under to see what was going on. She gently nibbled my hand but allowed me to continue.

Missy gives us a stretched-wing greeting as Sam looks on

Phyllis gets a "I'm Back" hug from Missy

As the months passed, Missy developed an enthusiastic penchant for playing with us. One day while Ralph was giving her a tummy rub, she stretched her body upright, held her head high, and trumpeted—not one or two but three commanding trumpet calls. That got Sam's immediate attention! He stopped eating and walked over to Missy. He responded with a trumpet call of his own, ending with a low timbre voice, much like the whinny of a horse, and then he lowered his head as though bowing before her.

As we silently watched, they nodded their heads in acceptance of the other's wooing. Standing chest to chest, the two swans began head-posturing. With necks straight, their heads turned from side to side in mirror-image movements, all the while looking intently at each other. Sam slightly flexed his wings outward but low in a display of courtship as they talked to one another in soft purr-like voices. Missy, impressed with Sam's courting technique, trumpeted again. In response, Sam displayed his swan nobility to a higher degree in an attempt to impress her further.

Soon they returned to the water and began courting. First they swam up to each other and nodded their heads in greeting. Then they came together, chest to chest, bills touching; forming the classic swan heart shape silhouette seen on greeting cards. First one trumpeted and the other answered. More head posturing followed. Next, each bird lowered its bill into the water and passionately blew bubbles. Again, they postured and trumpeted. Then, slowly they glided to a side by side position and postured cheek to cheek with heads high and necks straight. Sam was as regal as a cob could be, Missy the picture of stunning pen beauty. Gracefully, they swam away, except this time Missy was uncharacteristically in the lead.

"Wasn't that something to behold?" Ralph spoke in a hushed voice. It is extremely difficult to choose the perfect words to describe our feelings at that moment. Awe, delight, ecstasy, joy, and wonderment are a few that come quickly to mind. To have our presence accepted by the swans was an overwhelming experience.

Sam and Missy started molting in early July. Sam's wing feathers fell one at a time while Missy's primary wing feathers dropped two, three, or four at a time. Within two weeks Missy molted most of her primary and secondary wing feathers and lost the ability to fly. While flightless, Missy stayed in the water or very close to it at feeding times, ever alert to what was going on around her. When Missy did come ashore, she ate quickly, and then returned to the safety of the water with no interest in extended play visits.

"Have you noticed Sam hasn't lost all his wing feathers like Missy?" Ralph asked.

"You're right," I answered realizing that Sam had never molted all his feathers at one time. We had noticed that whenever new primary feathers grew on the injured wing, Sam worked on them until he had broken off all the long feathers, leaving only stubs. First, he stripped the barbs (the feathery texture of it) from the shaft. Then when only the bare shaft remained, Sam worked diligently to break each shaft off to a couple of inches in length. We can only wonder if he did this because the long primary feathers were uncomfortable over the wing stub.

"It must have something to do with his not being able to fly. He hasn't flown for so many years; maybe his internal clock senses this and no longer triggers the mechanism that causes a massive loss of wing feathers. Missy, because she flies, gets the molting process over quickly. I can't think of any other reason for the different molting patterns."

"We have seen Sam lose a lot of his smaller body feathers at one time," I answered, recalling finding Sam sitting on the marsh, surrounded by a large scattering of white feathers in the early summer months. Often we gathered the fallen feathers to give to the tree swallows the following spring.

Every April we put up nest boxes in the field for the tree swallows. We knew the tree swallows lined their nests with only white feathers. Each late May when the swallows began their nest construction, we often scattered smaller swan feathers around the bird boxes for them to use. At the end of each nesting season, we found an intricate grass nest lined with a circle of white feathers in each nesting box.

"There are no swallows flying," said a disappointed Ralph on one previous year's visit to the meadow.

"Let's wait a minute or two," I urged. "I see them flying over the duck pond."

Before long, one swallow flew over the field and landed on the nesting box. As the swallow watched, Ralph released a single white feather on the wind. The swallow swooped across the field, gathered the feather in midair, and flew into the nesting box with the treasure. Ralph released three more feathers. She carried the feathers into the birdhouse before flying off in search of a meal of flying insects.

"Let's spread the rest on the ground near the nesting box," Ralph suggested. As we left the field, we turned to see the swallow pick up one of the deposited feathers and take it in the box.

We have seen the swallows play with the white feathers while flying. A swallow would pick up a white feather lying in the grass. The bird flew upward, released the feather, then circled around and caught the feather as it floated downward. The tree swallow repeated the playful procedure. Sometimes, two or three swallows played the game together. While the game is in progress, the musical twitters of tree swallows filled the air.

We went home glad we could provide the swallows with white feathers for their nest and play.

Missy was flightless for about six weeks. First, small rounded evenly spaced projections resembling white straws appeared on her wings. When about an inch or more long, the tip of the white projections split and a minute feather tuft appeared. As the days passed, the tufts grew in length and width and soon were small versions of the larger primary and secondary wing feathers needed for flight. The stark white of the new feathers contrasted sharply against the older feathers.

"Missy's flying again," Ralph announced on a late August afternoon. She usually swam with Sam, hardly ever using her wings to move about the harbor. Whether she acquiesced in this because she knew Sam could not fly, we can only guess. That day, she vigorously flapped her wings, gained altitude, and skimmed across the harbor to the Old Landing. Had we just witnessed Missy's test flight of her new wing feathers?

During the summer of 1986, Sam and Missy became a twosome; where one was, the other was close by. When Missy disappeared behind a moored boat, Sam trumpeted to her with a tone of urgency in his voice. When Sam was out of her sight, Missy would stretch her long neck, turn her head from side to side, and swim around until she located him. Then, they greeted each other with soft purring voices. It seemed to us that the bond between them was strengthening. Since Missy returned to Sippican Harbor on her own and we fed them regularly, we hoped Missy had no reason to ever leave Sam. We were ecstatic with the prospect of Missy and Sam mating.

In September, I experienced another rapturous happenstance that I could not in my wildest imaginings have envisioned. On that day, the meal had ended and Missy was enjoying her playtime. Sam was in the water, waiting patiently for her to go with him. Missy was having too much fun to end her visit. "You are such a pretty swan," I spoke softly while gently stroking her long neck. As I rubbed her tummy, Missy stepped closer and closer to me until she was pushing against me. Since I was sitting on a stool, I could not move backwards. Her chest pressed against my face as she raised her body up high and gave a trumpet call. She kept trying to get even closer. Momentarily, I felt a large webbed foot land on my lap. Next, she nibbled my hair. Hoping to calm any anxiety she might feel, I gently enfold her in my arms and patted her back. Instantly, Missy's right foot was on my chest as she fought to maintain her balance. I HAD A SWAN ON MY LAP! As her long neck drooped over my right shoulder, I gently hugged her. Missy, not frightened by being on my lap, calmly let me touch her. I wondered if she was as puzzled as I on how we could separate.

When I felt Missy trying to climb higher, I leaned backward and to the left to allow her a chance to step off to the right. Once back on the sand, she turned and looked at me with a puzzled expression on her face.

Through the fall, Missy climbed on my lap a few more times. Before long, I became known as the Swan Lady. Missy loved to play and to be stroked after each feeding. It was quite a change from the don't-touch-me behavior when she first arrived in Sippican Harbor.

We know some people will doubt that swans can convey emotion by body language but we positively know they can. Our twenty-four year relationship with Sam and his friends has confirmed this. They can display anger, displeasure, and jealousy as well as acceptance, contentment and pleasure. We have seen these moods expressed by each of the swans we have known intimately.

Chapter Fifteen

A NEW YEAR'S CHANGE

Throughout October and November, we closely watched Missy for signs of a migration urge. Happily, we always found two swans waiting for us. Christmas came and went; still Missy stayed. By then, we felt sure that she intended to spend the winter with Sam.

Early on New Year's Day the birds were not waiting for us at the Old Landing. We scanned the empty harbor. It should have been easy to find two large white swans in an empty harbor, but it was not. At a distance, many of the white winter sticks that marked the locations of summer moorings could be mistaken for a swan's long neck.

"Missy's flying," I called, out looking through the binoculars. "She's headed towards the outer harbor." Was she just exercising her wings or beginning a migration flight?

In answer to our unheard question, Missy banked to the left and flew over Ram Island. Searching the water for Sam, I finally saw him floating in the middle of the harbor. With his head high, he watched Missy fly in a wide circle over the harbor. When Missy began a second flight circuit, Sam beat his wings frantically. He managed to raise two-thirds of his body up out of the water. His chest muscles contracted as he exerted greater power to his wings. Valiantly he fought to join his friend in flight. Unable to sustain the strenuous effort anymore, he sat back down on the water.

As Missy started another orbit over the harbor, Sam again began a frenzy of wing flapping as he struggled to get airborne. However, he failed to do the impossible. Completing a third fly-over loop of the harbor, Missy landed a few yards from Sam. He swam over to greet his high-flying friend as she began preening.

"Poor Sam! He wants to fly so badly and is unable to," Ralph said. "He has to feel terrible disappointment."

"I wish the man responsible for Sam's inability to fly would experience the failure that Sam just suffered." It was quite possible that there would be less careless hunting. A swan with only one wing equated to a man with only one arm or leg. Each life was drastically altered.

"We might as well go home. They aren't interested in eating yet."

At midmorning, we found the birds in Planting Island Cove when we searched the outer harbor from Silver Shell Beach. There was a third swan with them. Sam's wings were high as he swam at top speed, forcibly chasing the intruder.

At noontime we found only Sam waiting for us at the Old Landing. "Where's Missy?" I asked. Sam, acting uneasy, ate half of his meal then left. He trumpeted his 'worried where-are-you' call as he swam southward. His head turned left and right as he searched the empty harbor for Missy.

"She's gone. Sam failed the flight test earlier this morning," Ralph sorrowfully stated my silent thoughts. "She's flown off with the other mute." A swan who cannot fly is not a suitable mate. All the head dipping and nodding, bubble blowing and posturing did not mean a thing! "Poor Sam!"

All day long, we kept a check on our dejected swan. Sam searched many of the inlets in the harbor. Although he came for supper, he ate quickly and started searching again. Our hearts grieved for Sam and the emptiness he must be experiencing from Missy's departure.

We had learned two more facts about mute swans. First, swans migrate to open water as the ice forms and forces them out of their summer habitat. Second, Missy's urge to migrate for the winter was stronger than her attachment for Sam.

After a week or so, Sam gave up the obsession of searching for Missy. Then he took up a new position; he sat out in mid-channel off the boat ramp and bobbed in the water. It appeared that he wanted to be sure he was visible just in case Missy came back.

An Arctic cold front swept over us in late January, quickly freezing the harbor. Sam became stranded on the ice at Black Point. He just sat there in the swirling snow showers.

We checked on him often throughout the daylight hours, sure that he would become hungry enough to walk over the ice to the brook behind Daggett House. He had to know we would feed him there as we had the first winter.

"Sam, Sam," Ralph shouted across the frozen harbor later that afternoon trying to encourage the swan to come for supper. Darkness settled without any attempt from Sam to reach the brook. He spent the next day in the same spot. He did change sitting positions so we knew he was not stuck in the ice. We decided to wait for hunger to drive him to the brook. We felt sure Sam's body had enough winter fat to sustain him for another day.

"We've got to get to him," a worried Ralph announced when for the third day Sam made no effort to come for food. Three days without food or water did not seem wise for his safety. That night we made plans to reach Sam the following day.

"Hi, Charlie," I spoke over the telephone to our son. "Sam's stranded out on the ice."

"Where is he now?" Charlie asked.

"Off of Black Point. We'd like to move him to the boat yard where we can feed him daily. Could you give us a hand with the capture tomorrow?"

"Sure, what time do you need me?"

"I'll let you talk to Dad. He's already devised a rescue plan."

At noon the next day, we hiked across the same open marsh we had traversed to rescue Sam when he sustained the foot injury. This time, Charlie was carrying a huge cardboard box to transport the unsuspecting swan to his winter home. We tried to keep out of Sam's sight. Our fervent hope was not to alarm him and send him farther out on the ice. Since he was at the southern extension of Black Point, the scrub brush growing on the knob easily hid us from Sam's view. We reached our destination without Sam detecting our presence.

"Mom and I will coax Sam to shore with food," Ralph instructed. "When he is close enough for me to reach him, I'll slip the sheet over him. Then you come with the box."

"Good luck," whispered Charlie as we moved out into Sam's view.

"Sam," Ralph called to a surprised but a very attentive swan. The tail wiggled when he saw the food dish. This was a hungry bird. It did not take a lot of coaxing to get Sam to push himself over the ice. After much slipping, he finally inched to the dish and noisily gobbled down the food. We let Sam eat half of his meal just in case we failed in our attempt to capture him and he moved back out on the ice.

"Everything's all right," Ralph said soothingly to Sam as he quickly draped the sheet over the eating bird.

"We're ready for the box, Charlie," I called out, careful not to shout and frighten Sam. Charlie put the box down and quickly opened it. Swiftly, Ralph picked up the swan, placed him in the box, and lifted the sheet off the bird. Before Sam could make a move, Charlie folded the top over him. A rope secured the box to prevent a potentially angry swan from escaping.

Ten minutes later, we arrived at Sam's ideal winter home—the boat yard. Charlie untied the rope and opened the lid; Ralph lifted the rather tranquil swan from the box and set him down on the ground. Instantly, Sam knew where he was and headed down the icy shore to the open water surrounding the dock pilings.

"Sam seems happy to be in the water again," Charlie commented as the swan vigorously bathed away the three-day buildup of dirt. Once he finished cleaning to his satisfaction, we offered him food. He ate ravenously as though he just remembered that he hadn't eaten for three days.

"Now Sam, aren't you glad to be here? You won't have to be hungry or dirty," Ralph's voice was jubilant and relieved.

"It's good to have him here," I said, remembering how we worried when he was stranded on the ice. Sam's safety was a big concern of ours. He was a close friend, more than just a swan that we fed!

For the winter, Sam stayed at the boat yard. At night, he crawled up on the ice at the farther end of the dock to sleep. In February, as the days began to lengthen, Sam showed signs of cabin fever. Daily he swam the ever-enlarging southern boundary of his winter home. He did not know that a few hundred yards to the south the harbor was free from winter's icy grip.

"Now Sam, aren't you glad to be here? You won't have to be hungry or dirty,"

Chapter Sixteen

AN UNEXPECTED SPLASH

Once the ice disappeared, Sam returned to sitting out in the middle of the inner harbor off Black Point, facing southward. "Do you think he is expecting Missy to return?" I asked. "He's never sat in the same spot day after day."

"That's an explanation for his unusual behavior," Ralph said. "I doubt if we'll see Missy again. She left Sam to fly off with the other swan!"

Sam kept his faithful lookout throughout March and April. After eating, he swam back to the very same spot to command his lookout position. It distressed us to see him bobbing in the cold choppy water, but he didn't seem to mind.

Sam only broke off his sentry post to harass boats launched from the Old Landing. Although he failed to prevent the launchings, he continued his assault as he escorted the boat out to its mooring. His harassment seemed more intense that spring. Always, he returned to the same location off Black Point and waited (for what?) through sun and rain.

"The boat ramp's busy today," I commented when we arrived for an afternoon feeding in late May. One boat was almost ready to move down the ramp while three others waited in parade formation for their turn.

"Everyone is taking advantage of the tide. Sam's swimming in battle formation marking his territorial boundary-line between the end of the south wharf and the end of the old stone pier," Ralph said, giving meaning to Sam's swimming in a straight line between the two points. "Do you suppose he's claiming all the harbor on the other side of that invisible line as his territory?"

"Watch Sam," Ralph instructed as a truck, trailer, and boat with a man aboard started backing down the ramp. Sam fiercely charged at the boat with his long neck and head folded between his raised wings and fire in his eyes. As the boat slid from the trailer, Sam circled about and charged at it again. The man pushed the starter button on the engine hoping for a smooth beginning of his boating season. However, the engine did not cooperate and the boat drifted aimlessly with the sluggish current.

"Sam's going to get hurt unless we get him away from that boat," a worried Ralph declared. "I'm going out on the old stone pier to coax him to come and eat. That man is having so much trouble with that stubborn engine he isn't thinking about Sam's safety." Ralph started to walk out on the old pier. "Sam's so determined to evict that boat I'm not sure he'll come. See if you can get him ashore near the stone pier. Once he starts eating corn bread, maybe he'll forget about the boat."

Before long, people gathered to observe the problematical launch. A dubious launching attracted the 'native gulls', the name given to the shell fishermen that gathered most spring evenings to enjoy a round of talk about boating, fishing and local politics. At times the topic of conversation was the rehashing of difficult launches at the Old Landing. I felt sorry for the man with the stubborn engine. I knew he'd be the topic for that evening's gathering of the 'native gulls.'

Sam ignored Ralph's calls. The boat with its frustrated owner drifted ever closer to the unintimidated swan. Again, the man turned the ignition key as Sam charged the stern with the engine; neither the man nor swan seemed to know where the other was or the looming danger lurking.

"Bring the corn bread out here. "HURRY" Ralph shouted. "Maybe the sight of it will make Sam forget the boat and remind him he is hungry."

"I'm coming," I stepped out on the stone pier as Sam started to answer Ralph's calls. However, when he saw the corn bread I was offering, he changed course and swam toward me. His forward speed created a wake.

As he swam closer, his neck stretched to it fullest length and the bill opened wide to receive the food. I bent down from a standing position to hand the corn bread to Sam. Suddenly I lost my balance. For a split second, I felt I had recovered my equilibrium. A split second later, I realized I was about to tumble into the water.

As I pitched downward, I saw Sam in full retreat; his large feet churned the water and his wings beat frantically as he fought to reverse his forward speed to escape the impending catastrophe.

With a loud attention-getting splash, I landed in the water. I sat up and looked about to see if Sam was all right. Sam was now out beyond the stone pier still watching me with a fight-or-flight look in his eyes!

"Are you all right?" Ralph asked.

"It's too early to go swimming," said the man in the boat.

"I'm okay," I answered as I reached to retrieve the shoe that was floating seaward. I felt the weight of my waterlogged jacket, the matted wet hair and the rivulets of water running down my face. What a funny picture I must have presented to the 'gulls.' I was not physically hurt but my dignity had not fared so well. Now I would be the topic for discussion at the next gathering of the 'gulls.'

Poor Sam, I thought. Would he understand that I had not wanted to hurt him, that my fall was an accident?

"Can you get up?" Ralph asked, fearing I might have suffered an injury.

My dignity suffered a second blow when I stood up and the water line was only knee deep. Ralph helped me up on to the pier.

Then we turned our attention to Sam to see how we could calm his fears. At first, Sam swam towards us but soon his fear seemed to overrule his desire for food and he turned away. He retreated farther out into the harbor.

"You've got to get into dry clothes," Ralph suggested. "It will take time for Sam to overcome his fright. Besides, there will be less boat activity later."

"I really need a shower!" I carried the aroma of rank marsh mud flavored with a whiff of gasoline fumes.

Returning later, we found Sam eating marsh grass at the Old Landing beach. The people had gone since the ebbing tide now made it impossible to launch skiffs at the boat ramp.

"I'll stay in the car until he comes out to eat," I suggested. "He probably won't come if he sees me."

I watched as Ralph patiently coaxed Sam to his food dish. Five minutes later I decided to join the swan and Ralph on the beach. The swan was unconcerned with my approach until I was within five feet.

"Sam, where are you going," Ralph asked as he placed himself between the swan and the water.

"Cronk," Sam voiced his protest. However, the wings did not rise in alarm. "Cronk," he repeated as he stepped back and then to the side to circumvent Ralph.

"I wish I hadn't tried to join you. It probably strengthens the imprint of my fall in Sam's memory."

"Sam will soon forget today's events," Ralph consoled. "You'll see."

Two days later, Sam visited us while we were aboard the Cygnus Olor. I stayed out of sight until Ralph fed him a few pieces of the favored corn bread. Slowly, I moved into view but there was no reaction from the swan. Then I decided to test Sam's memory of two days ago. I leaned over the side and hand-offered Sam some corn bread. Without hesitation Sam took the food, and then ate two more pieces before he hastily retreated.

"What made him swim away?" I asked since neither of us had moved.

"Maybe he just remembered your fall into the water. Or maybe he was spooked by his reflection in the waxed hull. That's another question without an answer."

A week later we decided to test the depth of Sam's trust in me. Ralph stayed in the car while I walked down the beach to feed him. To alleviate any fears Sam might have, I discarded the purple jacket I had worn on the day of the fall. I put on the old beige coat I wore at the very beginning of our relationship.

From past experiences, we knew Sam appeared to react to colors in different ways. When I wore my red slacks, he seemed to back off from me. I never wore red to visit Sam. Maybe my muted purple jacket that I wore on the day of my 'early swim' was unacceptable clothing to wear when visiting Sam.

"Hello Sam," I greeted my swan friend as I tossed a piece of corn bread to him. Sam charged up the beach, stopped long enough to eat the tossed cornbread and then took bread from my hand. Relief flooded through me, Sam had forgotten our distressing encounter of ten days ago! At that moment, I realized how much I had missed being with him these past days.

Finishing the bread, Sam grabbed my sleeve making the usual honking sound requesting 'more bread please.' I stroked his long neck and for a few minutes everything was amicable. When he tried to come closer, he bumped into my knee and instantly things changed. Sam panicked; his body tensed, the head and neck came up and he moved towards the water. Our joyful reunion ended!

"Well, what do you think?" I asked returning to the car.

"When Sam walked up to you, he carried his head low and the wings rose a little. It was almost the same posture he displayed to Missy and Little One last year when he was telling them of his displeasure. He was telling you not to get too close. I didn't notice anything unusual to make him go back into the water so quickly."

"I think he startled himself when he bumped into my knee. Our trusting relationship is beginning to return to where it was before the fall."

A few weeks later as I got out of the car in the village parking lot a jovial voice asked, "Did you enjoy your early swim?"

"I've often thought I might try to swim with Sam to see how he'd react," I answered. "However, I wouldn't have chosen to swim in May nor would I have done it with an audience."

Maybe some summer day I'll try that swim with Sam. However, I would not don a bathing suit; I would protect myself by wearing clothing with long sleeves and pants. There was no predicting what Sam's reaction would be. Would he perceive me as a sea monster to vanquish in a mighty battle?

Chapter Seventeen

GREAT JOY

By the middle of June, Sam gave up his persistent watch for Missy's return. At the same time, our tiny glimmer of hope that Missy might return ended. If she did not return in February, March, or April at the height of mating season, there appeared to be little reason to expect her to come back in June. Sam reverted to his bachelor habits of dozing in the sun, unhurried meals with play time, and journeys about the harbor; going where he wanted when he wanted.

Another surprise awaited us when we arrived the morning on June 30. There were two swans! Sam was preening on the marsh bank while the other was feeding in the brook.

"Now, which swan is with Sam?" Ralph wondered aloud. "There's no aggression between them so he knows the swan. It must be Missy."

"It might not be," I cautioned. Neither swan had seen us yet.

"Missy," Ralph shouted as he clapped his hands. The newly arrived swan started to swim toward us. "It is Missy, she's coming" his voice was filled with exuberance. No other swan would answer our hand-clapping signal. "She's not waiting for Sam. Who would have thought she'd come back this late in the season?"

"Missy!" Ralph greeted the swan as she came ashore. She gave him a head nod and went straight to the feeding dish. "It's Missy! There's a hole in the webbed skin of the left foot. No two swans could have a hole in the exact same spot."

When Sam finally came to eat, he didn't seem angry that Missy was eating from his dish. He appeared to be on his best behavior, letting her eat first. When she slowed down, they took turns eating from the dish.

Was it an attachment to Sam that brought Missy back or was it the food? If it was the first, why hadn't she come during mating season? Definitely, we had more to learn about mute swans.

Later, we delved into research and found a possible answer. She was still an adolescent! Mutes do not choose a mate until they are four or five years old. Her relationship with Sam was strictly platonic. What about Sam? Would he have felt platonic or amorous towards his Missy when the spring mating urges flowed? At the end of June, however, he seemed happy to have her back. We were overjoyed to have Missy and Sam together again.

"I feel the notch in her lower front bill," Ralph said as Missy nibbled his finger. For us, Missy answering Ralph's hand-clap, her walking up the beach and the head nod she gave him was all it took for us to positively identify her. A skeptical person may not accept that fact on such little proof. However, the additional evidence of the hole in the web of the left foot and the broken notch in the bill had to convince an unbeliever.

We left when the swans returned to the brook. A noontime check found the swans side by side on Sam's favorite rock. Missy was asleep while Sam kept watch. He had a happy and contented aura about him as he guarded his sleeping friend. Our happiness matched Sam's.

"Oh, look what's coming!" Ralph said at the end of an afternoon feeding a few days later. Missy had just returned to the water to join the patiently waiting Sam.

Turning my head, I saw Mother Mallard with six downy-soft ducklings trailing in a neat line behind her, silently swimming towards us along the Knowlton House breakwater. The water rippled gently in an ever-widening vee-formation as mother duck swam to the tossed corn. We were awed that Mother Mallard considered our presence acceptably safe enough to bring her babies to feed.

Upon reaching the corn, the silence was broken with a mixed chorus of peeps from the baby ducks as the single file formation ended. The mother duck began eating in the shallow water. Soon the ducklings were imitating her eating, although without her expertise. Two of the babies reached for the same kernel of corn only to bump heads. Each jerkily backed off, peeping loudly. This appeared to be an eating lesson as Mother Mallard continually talked to her brood in between bites of corn.

"No, Missy," I commanded in a firm voice as Missy raised her wings slowly and swam towards the ducks. Sam calmly watched from a distance. The ever-alert duck had also seen Missy's warning signal, and quacked loudly as she ordered her ducklings to follow her. Soon mother and ducklings formed a solid mass of heads, bills, and feathers; all silently moving in complete unison as if controlled by a single brain.

Reaching the marsh grass growing at the water edge, Mother Mallard sent her ducklings into hiding amongst the tall green mass. As they safely disappeared, mother duck turned and faced the advancing swan. Missy, menacing with her fully raised wings, swam towards Mother Mallard who was standing at full attention, angrily quacking at the approaching swan, not in the least intimidated by Missy's larger size! It was then that the duck revealed true courage. Quacking loudly, mother duck fluttered towards a surprised Missy, who stopped advancing. Next, she landed on Missy's back while her quacking increased in volume and intensity. A startled Missy slapped the water with her wings, creating bass crescendos to the Mallard's quacking.

"Well, I'll be darned," Ralph whispered. Breathlessly we watched, fascinated by the drama being played out in front of us.

The volume of the battle would have led one to expect to see feathers flying in every direction. However, as quickly as the assault began, it was over. The Mallard flew off Missy's back and ended the conflict. She landed near the marsh where her brood was hidden and flapped her wings in victory. The ducklings emerged from the marsh grass, circling her completely as each vied to get the closest to their mother. In a minute or two, Mother Duck and her brood headed back to the scattered corn. A chorus of tiny peeps filled the air as the duck family settled down to finish the interrupted meal.

"Look at Missy," Ralph called out. "She is having a super bath. Maybe she is trying to wash off any invisible trace of mother duck being on her back."

We had never seen Missy bathe so meticulously. When she dipped her head deeply under water, her body was almost completely immersed. Then she resurfaced and sent the seawater coursing down her back. With final abandon, Missy rolled over sideways; one circular rollover rotation followed by another and yet another. Once upright again, she rhythmically beat her wings and sent sprays of water showering over her. She followed this by flapping her wings in a long sustained flutter that raised her body almost completely out of the water. A few minutes later, she settled back down on the water surface and began to preen her feathers.

"Sam's never done that," Ralph's voice was filled with awe. "Probably he can't roll himself over in the water because of the uneven balance of his body. Maybe that missing outer third of the left wing has limited more than Sam's flying ability."

The summer of 1987 was one of pure serenity for the swans and us. Early mornings of quiet breakfasts and tranquil evening mealtimes were spent with the swans. We experienced great pleasure when the swans visited the Cygnus Olor while we were aboard. We would be sitting and reading when a gentle tap-tap sounded against the hull. Peeking over the side, we would find the two swans waiting for a handout.

Chapter Eighteen

DETERMINATION

During late fall we watched Missy closely for signs of a migration urge. Although the two swans were together constantly, now Missy displayed a slight aloofness towards Sam. We noticed a decrease in her inclination to follow him.

"Have you noticed that Missy isn't playing with us as much as she did during the summer?" Ralph asked at an afternoon feeding in mid November.

"No," I answered. "Come to think of it, she doesn't seem to want tummy rubs. But, Sam still seems to enjoy playing with you as much as ever."

"She hasn't given any trumpet calls either," Ralph added.

Two days later, we found Sam all alone! Had Missy migrated earlier this year? Did she leave by herself or had she joined other migrating swans? To our surprise, Sam did not seem as upset by this year's departure. Had Missy, during their soft purring conversations, communicated her plans to leave to him?

With only Sam to feed, our daily feeding visits settled into a quiet routine. In early January, ice began to cover the harbor and Sam was caught on the southern edge of it. The ice crept across the harbor from north to south, pushing Sam farther and farther seaward.

"We have to find a way to capture Sam before the ice pushes him further out," Ralph said when the ice edge reached Nye's wharf. "Another few days and Sam will be forced too far out for us to reach him."

"Could we use a skiff to reach him?" I asked.

"A skiff won't be of any use. The ice along the shore will be too thick to get through."

The next morning we found Sam hemmed in by thin ice some distance from shore. Later in the day, the ice melted to slush. He pushed himself through it to reach a beach between two private docks.

"He seems uneasy in this strange area," Ralph said as Sam refused to come on shore.

Over breakfast the next morning, we made plans to move Sam to the boatyard. It was the perfect winter home for him. We could feed him daily and he would have open water for bathing.

That morning Sam appeared to be very hungry as he eagerly walked ashore at the beach to the south of Nye's wharf. Ralph bent down and picked up the swan. There was no protesting honk from the bird. Seconds later, a surprised but subdued Sam was sitting beside me in the back of the car.

"Should you cover Sam's head?" Ralph asked as he started the car.

"No need. He's just sitting and looking out the window."

After a short ride we arrived at the boatyard. The men, seeing Sam sitting in the back seat of the car, stopped shoveling snow, smiled, and waved as they watched their guest arrive to spend the winter. Sam had spent many winters at the boatyard over the years.

Sam seemed contented with our decision to move him to the boat yard. As thick ice covered the inner harbor; it appeared that the 1987-88 winter was to be very ordinary.

However, soon Sam proved us wrong, again. That winter we learned just how determined he could be once he decided to do something. Sam was not a swan to be easily discouraged from a chosen course of action once he decided what he wanted to do.

One February morning I stopped for a midmorning check on Sam. I found him walking over the ice, halfway between the boat yard and the north wharf at the Old Landing, heading southeast towards Black Point.

Why, I wondered, was he leaving an 'ideal' winter home at the boat yard for the cold hard ice that awaited him at Black Point? Sam seemed very determined—he would walk four or five steps and then sit on the ice to rest. Minutes later, he would struggle to get up on his feet then walk a few steps and sit again. It took him all morning, but by noon he reached Black Point.

"Sam, you need to walk back to the boat yard," Ralph instructed when we found him sitting on the ice off Black Point at noon. "Going there makes no sense at all."

"Now where is he headed?" I asked, surprised to see Sam get up on his feet and begin to walk once more.

"He's heading towards Hammett Cove," Ralph said as Sam rounded Black Point and headed eastward." Sam's actions were puzzling to us. "He's going farther away from his perfect winter home."

At 2:00 p.m., I found Sam still journeying to his unknown destination. Now he was half walking and half-swimming in the high tide water that edged the shoreline. I drove to Tabor's wharf to watch as Sam continued his mystery hike over the ice.

With the binoculars, I watched Sam's slow progress along the shoreline. By chance, I looked into Hammett Cove to see if there was open water. As I looked at the sparkling blue water, two swans swam from behind the breakwater. That must be the reason for Sam's long journey over the ice. Sam must have seen them land earlier in the morning and was determined to join or evict them! The ice was a barrier to be conquered one step at a time. Although he could not see them as he hiked over the ice, he must have remembered their arrival. It was not a case of 'out of sight, out of mind!'

"We didn't expect to be feeding Sam in Hammett Cove this year," Ralph commented as we walked over the same field we traversed every day two winters ago. "Will we have three swans to feed today?"

However, one lone swan wiggled his tail in greeting upon our arrival. Sam had successfully encouraged the two visitors to leave.

"Well Sam, you've eaten all the cornbread." As Sam held on to his shirtsleeve, Ralph gently stroked the underside of the swan's neck. Sam stood still, mesmerized by the gentle caresses. "It would be great if you would walk back to the boat yard tomorrow," Ralph suggested.

That would have been nice for us but Sam had other plans. He stayed in Hammett Cove for the rest of the winter. We wondered if he was keeping the cove for Missy and himself when she returned in the spring. Sam seemed faithful to his absent partner. Was Missy being as unerringly loyal to Sam on her winter hiatus?

By the end of February the ice melted completely and Sam returned to the Old Landing area. He persistently harassed each launched boat, reminding the boaters that they were entering HIS harbor. Again, he repeated his steadfast waiting for Missy's return.

Chapter Nineteen

BABE

For six weeks, Sam swam in the water near the Old Landing and Black Point, waiting for Missy's return. On the morning of April 27, we found two swans swimming off Black Point.

"Missy's back," I shouted joyfully. However, my joy was short lived, for the swan that followed Sam was not Missy. The newest arrival was a young bird still showing a mottling of brown feathers just like Missy's when she first arrived.

"It's a young pen," Ralph said. "The knob is smaller than Missy's and Sam's. I'd guess the age to be two or three years." Sam's willing acceptance of the little swan's presence puzzled us.

"We should give our new bird a name," I suggested a few days later when the swan was still with Sam. We always considered the naming of a swan a major decision, comparable to the naming of our children. After careful deliberation, we chose Babe as the perfect name.

Sam no longer waited for Missy's return. Where Sam went, Babe tagged along. Quickly, she learned to eat cracked corn from a dish. We had mixed feelings about the friendship developing between the swans. We wondered what Missy's reaction would be when she found another swan with her Sam. We did expect her to return to spend the summer with Sam. Since Missy probably would not return until mid-June at the earliest, we decided to enjoy interacting with Sam and Babe.

Arriving on a day in late May, we found a third swan swimming near the beach at the Old Landing while Sam and Babe were grazing on sea grass in Daggett House Brook. Missy was back!

"Missy, Missy," Ralph called excitedly when the newest arrival reacted to the blinking of the car lights by swimming to shore. Without hesitation, she walked up the beach to greet us.

"Let's get her fed before Sam discovers what we are doing," Ralph suggested. Missy remembered everything; she watched as we brought the food from the car and came forward when we placed the dish on the beach. Noisily, she slurped up the bread and corn.

"Here comes trouble," Ralph announced as Sam swam around the breakwater with Babe tagging along. Missy, seeing Sam approach, walked farther up the beach. However, it appeared she did not want to escape.

"Sam, cornbread," Ralph called out as he set up the feeding dish, hoping to cool the swan's disapproval of seeing another swan on the beach. Sam swam along the water's edge, looking big and bad with his wings fully extended, head back and glaring at Missy. Not intimidated, she vigilantly watched Sam, determined to remain on the beach. Sam conceded the battle was a standoff and began to eat.

"Sam, don't you know it is Missy?" Ralph asked. "Babe is staying safely in the water; she knows what is happening between the other two and wants no part of it." When Sam left after eating, Babe followed him. Then, Missy came, ate, and left.

The following morning, all three swans were waiting at the boat ramp. Sam and Babe floated nearer to shore while Missy was farther out on the water. Missy, seeing us, headed for the beach. Sam, seeming to object, chased her away with his wings raised and his head down in an aggressive stance. Fifty feet from shore, Sam halted the chase and returned to Babe.

"Let's feed them while we can," I suggested, deciding we would find a way to feed Missy later.

However, she decided not to wait. While the other two swans were busy eating, Missy quietly came ashore on the opposite side of the boat ramp. While Ralph fed her, I kept Sam and Babe occupied.

Before long, Sam noticed Missy's presence and immediately entered the water to evict her. Missy hurriedly returned to the water and quickly swam away with Sam in hot pursuit. Babe looked at the feuding swans but continued to eat. Once Babe finished eating she did not join Sam in the chase. She swam to the shallow water and began looking for grass.

After Sam chased Missy roughly three hundred yards from shore, he swam back to Babe and started grassing. Missy, content to stay out among the boats, began to preen and before long, she was asleep.

To our dismay, the evening meal was a repeat of the morning. Sam appeared determined not to allow Missy to come to eat. By being persistent, Missy finally outwitted Sam and gained a foothold on the beach. Babe seemed unconcerned by the struggle between the other two swans. Although Sam and Missy ate, each kept a cautious eye on the other. Sam returned to the water when he finished eating, but placed himself where he could watch Missy. He appeared ready to chase her once she entered the water. Missy bided her time. Seeing her chance, she quickly walked to the water, entered and swam away at top speed. As Sam got closer, she flapped her powerful wings and skimmed over the water to escape the charging swan. For a while Missy was an ostracized swan with Sam preferring Babe's company.

"Where are Babe and Missy?" Ralph asked when we found Sam alone one morning. Scanning the harbor, we did not locate the missing swans.

"Sam's not too concerned with their disappearance." He was calmly eating his breakfast. We expected Missy might leave since Sam ignored her but, Babe's departure puzzled us.

Four days later Missy came back—ALONE!

"Where's Babe?" I asked her. "Didn't she want to come back with you?"

"Missy knows how to take care of the competition," Ralph remarked. "She took Babe for a flight and probably lost her in a flock of swans. Then she flew away when Babe wasn't watching. Now she has Sam all to herself."

However, there was still upheaval in Sam and Missy's relationship. Now, Missy claimed the beach her private territory and would not let Sam come to eat there. One day when he approached the beach, she angrily chased after him with her large wings loudly striking the surface of the water as she skimmed over it. She caught Sam, grabbed the back of his neck in her bill, and held on as she thrashed him with her wings. The noise was deafening but the action was not deadly. Breaking away from Missy's hold, Sam quickly swam away in defeat.

Missy seemed to enjoy her newfound power! Sam deferred to her wishes and kept his distance. We had mixed feelings about the situation. We felt bad when Sam ignored Missy upon her return, and delighted when she removed Babe. At first we even found it tolerable when she started to give Sam a dose of his own uppity behavior. However, we soon began to feel sorry for our Sam bird!

The relationship returned to normal a few days later. Sam swam around Missy to reach the other side of the beach. As an added unspoken statement, he held his wings only slightly raised. There was no reaction from Missy. Was it possible Missy now wanted to be friends again? That day Sam was forgiven. The two swans seemed to pick up where the relationship had ended the previous fall.

However, Missy was a changed swan—no longer did she accept Sam's tendency to be the domineering mate. When she appeared to reach the end of her patience, she would let him have a wing or two. Sam, with no Babe around to swim with, accepted the new Missy. Throughout the summer, sometimes Sam was the leader while at other times Missy was the boss bird!

Chapter Twenty

MISSY FLIES THE COOP

"Missy's flying to the Old Landing." I marveled at the gracefulness of the swan in flight under the late October sun. Since the beginning of fall, Missy flew three or four times a week on short flights around the harbor.

"Sam's coming, he's paddling as fast as he can," Ralph said. "He doesn't like it when she leaves him behind." As he swam in the direction that Missy had flown, his long neck was straight as an arrow and the erect head turned constantly as he searched for his Missy. He called in a bark-like voice that seemed to plead 'where are you' as he continued his pursuit.

"Do you suppose Missy's trying to coax Sam into the air," Ralph asked.

"She must know by now that Sam cannot fly." I answered. "Do you think she can comprehend why he can't fly?"

"Ornithologists tell us swans cannot rationalize," Ralph said. "But who really knows for sure. They claim birds, swans included, only react to what is happening around them."

I wondered if that was true, as I recalled that Sam remembered the two swans that landed in Hammett Cove last winter and determinedly walked there to evict them when he could no longer see them. That desire was so strong that he spent five hours walking over slippery ice to chase them out of his harbor.

A week later, on a mid-morning stop at the Old Landing, I found the birds still on the beach. Missy had her head tucked under her wing while Sam was alert. Since both ate well at breakfast time, I did not stop to offer a tidbit.

At noon, Ralph reported that he did not see either swan at the Old Landing. Since it was such a warm sunny day, we expected that the birds were on a sojourn; probably dining on algae growing on some of the moorings. Swans love green veggies!

When I met Ralph at the Old Landing at four-thirty, no swans were waiting to be fed.

"Let's go down to Tabor's dock and check there," Ralph suggested after a search with the binoculars did not locate the missing swans.

"I'll drive down to the town dock to look for them and meet you at Tabor," I said. "I'll look with the binoculars toward Planting Island cove. Maybe they are on their way in."

From the town dock I saw a lone Sam swimming up the center of the harbor; his posture and actions told me that he was searching for Missy. My heart broke as I observed through the binoculars, but did not hear, Sam call for Missy. Had she left Sam again?

By the time I returned to Tabor's dock, Ralph had also seen Sam and realized Missy had gone. As we watched, Sam swam past the dock headed toward the Old Landing boat ramp for his evening meal. Although we were aware that there was a good chance that Missy would leave, it was still hard to accept. How could she leave her Sam so easily? How could she leave the daily feedings offered so regularly? Missy probably left sometime during the afternoon, flying in a southward direction and Sam swam south looking for her. How far out of the harbor had Sam gone before he gave up the search? Was it the falling darkness and the thoughts of his evening meal that made Sam return to the Old Landing or did he just give up the search for the missing Missy?

"He's swimming at top speed," Ralph observed. "He's in full battle position."

At the water's edge Sam stopped momentarily, and then swam parallel to shore with his wings still fully raised. It appeared that Sam was displaying to us his displeasure over Missy's departure.

"Come Sam," I coaxed the apparently unhappy swan. Finally he ate and quickly left. As he swam away, he called for the missing friend. When he received no answer, Sam swam to the brook in the gathering dusk. He stopped twenty feet from shore and began to preen his feathers. From his mannerisms, we believed Missy had been gone for some time; otherwise, Sam would still be searching. The fact that he stationed himself in open water was an indication to us that he wanted to be visible just in case Missy returned.

"Let's wait awhile, Missy may come back," I suggested.

"Missy won't be back. She's some distance away otherwise she would be here for the much loved goldfish-shaped crackers."

In the past few weeks, Missy had developed a keen taste for those little crackers. Ralph and I laughed at the expression on Missy's face when he brought the plastic bag of favored crackers from the bread wrapper. She intently followed the course of that bag and stretched her long neck in the same direction. When Ralph took a goldfish-shaped cracker from the bag and slowly moved it up to his mouth and popped it in, Missy's facial expression was one of puzzlement and perplexity. I know it will be hard for a casual bird observer to believe, but these two swans did show facial expressions.

The next morning there was only one swan waiting for breakfast. While we had not expected to find Missy with Sam that morning, secretly we each hoped she would be there.

"You have to come to us to eat," I said to the obstinate swan. Sam appeared just as insistent on having his meal come to him. We compromised; he came to the waterline, and we placed his dish in front of him. Just because he was the only swan did not mean that things would always go his way. Winter was coming; we wanted our relationship to remain strong so we could feed Sam when he needed our food the most. Breakfast was over without much ceremony.

"Oh Sam," I called out as I heard him trumpet for his missing friend. Although we wanted to ease Sam's loneliness, there was little we could do. He had to work his way through this separation. Because mute swans mate for life, we felt Sam was experiencing some 'feelings' of separation and loss. Although I knew that mute swans could not rationalize like us humans, there had to be some sense of feelings, otherwise why did they choose one mate to be attached to for life?

"Missy's back," Ralph shouted when he returned from working on our mooring later that morning. "She and Sam are preening their feathers on the beach. Let's go feed her."

"You're a hungry girl," Ralph said when Missy's head was in the dish before he placed it on the ground. "From the way she's eating her corn, I'd say she didn't eat too well yesterday."

We wondered where she had spent the night. Had she flown non-stop from there to here for her breakfast? What prompted her to return to Sippican Harbor? Was it food, a sense of returning to home, or the need for Sam's companionship? These were more questions that we would never be able to answer.

"Have you noticed how Sam is on his best behavior?" Ralph questioned. Sam appeared pleased to have Missy back. All thoughts of rivalry appeared forgotten. Sam was probably feeling some form of swan contentment.

Sam's and our happiness was short lived. Two days later, Missy left again and this time she did not return. Missy was on her winter hiatus.

As any fisherman would probably tell you, a harbor never freezes over in the same pattern two years in a row. Sam was on the boatyard side when ice formed between Black Point and the south dock at the Old Landing. However, our prospects of an easy winter caring for our swan changed with a January cold spell.

"Sam can't come to eat," Ralph said the next morning when we found the ice had formed along the boatyard shoreline. Sam was swimming in the open water under the wooden dock where the fans had churned all night.

"Let's coax him to walk over the ice to shore," I suggested.

Sam did not approve of that idea. He just swam back and forth along the ice edge that separated us.

"Let's walk out on the dock and drop food down to him," Ralph suggested next. Sam almost seemed to read our minds, for he was swimming toward the dock as we walked out on it. Breakfast consisted of bread and cornbread that morning.

"I can attach strings to the four-corners of Sam's feeding dish holder," Ralph suggested that evening. "Then we can lower the corn and water dish down to him from the dock."

"I know swans can drink salt water but it would be nice to offer Sam fresh water."

The next morning Sam seemed puzzled when he bumped his head on the strings attached to his dish. After a few tries, he figured out how

to drink the water and avoid the strings. Sam appeared to relish the fresh water as much as we thought he would. Windy days presented a new challenge of getting the dish down to Sam before the wind sloshed the water out. Ralph became very proficient at dropping cornbread pieces into the dish below. While we missed stroking and playing with Sam at mealtime, we felt elation just to be able to feed him daily.

Chapter Twenty-One

A DIFFERENT SUMMER RELATIONSHIP

With the change of the season, Sam moved back to the Old Landing area. We were delighted to be able to play with him at mealtime. This year he was not as dedicated to watching for Missy. Soon the boats launched at the Old Landing boat ramp took all his attention.

"Sam got pulled under a boat being launched," a man told us one morning when we arrived to feed him. "He swam over to the brook after he bobbed up." He pointed to where Sam was sitting on shore, twitching his wings—first one then the other, and preening his feathers. "I'm not sure if he was injured or not."

With a quick thank you, we drove over to see how Sam was for ourselves. The feathers were white—no blood showing anywhere. Ralph gently picked Sam up to see if he was injured underneath—no blood. It was when Ralph examined his legs and feet that he found the injury—a scrape on the bottom of his left foot.

"What a lucky bird!" The tone of Ralph's voice was filled with the immense relief he felt.

"If swans, like cats, have nine lives, Sam just used another one," I joked as the enormity of what the outcome of this accident could have been released its hold on me.

"I don't think Sam needs to see Dr. Tremblay," Ralph broke into my thoughts. "It appears that only the skin was scraped off the pad, no injury to the bone itself. It should scab over in a few days."

As Sam ate breakfast, we tried to think of ways to protect him from his instinct to charge at newly-launched boats. With a child, one can reprimand and lecture, but how do you teach a swan about safety?

Ralph thought of one possibility. Within a week, the town placed a sign at the boat ramp instructing boaters to be careful of the swan when starting boat engines. Now, boaters were aware of Sam's presence. The sign itself stated that Sam was a member of the community, so boaters should use extra caution for his safety when launching a boat. It was the best solution humanly possible.

Sam recovered and life settled into a pleasant routine. Our visits with him were delightful interludes. He seemed to enjoy them too—he was never in a hurry to leave. We half expected to find Missy with Sam at one of the feedings. When May arrived and Missy had not returned, we felt sure she had found herself a handsome cob during the winter and would not return to summer with Sam.

Much to our surprise, on a mid-May feeding we found a swan sitting on the Old Landing beach. "Missy," Ralph greeted the swan.

She must have recognized her name, or Ralph's voice, for she arose and walked toward us. Before we got the food out of the car she was walking over the pavement to the car. Sam was sitting in the water just observing Missy. "Sam, you don't act very happy to have your Missy back," I said. "Cornbread, Sam" I coaxed. He made no effort to come. "Do you suppose he is upset that Missy is already on the beach?"

"Maybe he chased her up here," Ralph gave one explanation. "We'll feed her first. He might charge up to his dish when she starts slurping corn."

Once Missy finished eating, she sat down on the beach to preen.

"Come Sam," Ralph called as he placed his dish in the water. Slowly, very slowly, he swam over to eat. He never did get out of the water that afternoon. Was it possible that Sam did not realize it was Missy sitting there?

The interaction between Sam and Missy on the day of her return proved to be a foretelling of their 1989 summer relationship.

"Sam's coming," Ralph said as we watched Missy fly to the Old Landing for supper one late September afternoon.

"I see him," I answered. "He appears to be searching for Missy." I shouted and clapped my hands, giving the customary signal that his meal was waiting. At that moment he must have seen Missy on shore for his forward speed increased.

"Missy is flying a lot lately," Ralph commented. "Do you suppose she's preparing for her migration flight?"

"It's too soon for her to migrate. Maybe she'll stay with Sam this winter." Secretly, my romantic nature hoped Missy would stay with her Sam.

"She has no way of knowing that we feed Sam all winter, so survival instincts nudge her to fly to open water," Ralph, ever the realist that balanced my romantic inclinations, suggested the real reason Missy left for the winter.

Of course, Ralph was right. Besides, she had returned twice since that first summer spent with Sam, so there was no reason to believe she would not return next spring.

I had read that mute swans mate in February or early March. It seemed to me that May or June was too late for Sam and Missy to start a family. Maybe they were not the bonded pair I thought they had become.

"Sam, come back," I ordered as he walked over to Missy's feeding dish. When he began to eat her food, Missy calmly walked to Sam's dish and ate. A minute later, Sam came back to eat from his dish and Missy returned to her own.

"Lately, Sam appears upset when I feed Missy," Ralph commented. "She doesn't seem to mind who is feeding her, as long as there is food in the dish"

Mealtime had evolved from a close-knit foursome to a definite separate table affair. We set their feeding dishes some distance apart since Sam sometimes acted aggressively towards Missy. We even switched off between the two swans; one meal Ralph fed Missy and I fed Sam, then the next time he served Sam while I fed her.

That afternoon, when Ralph rubbed Missy's tummy, she raised her head and gave a commanding trumpet call that ended with a short trill. Sam's head came up from his dish and his wings rose slightly; he lumbered over to Ralph and Missy with his head hung low in an aggressive manner.

"Sam, what's wrong," a surprised Ralph asked as the swan deliberately walked between him and Missy.

"My guess is that he doesn't want Missy near you." I ventured. Sam appeared not satisfied with just separating them; he seemed determined to move Missy away from Ralph.

"He's never done that before." Ralph replied.

Once Sam successfully forced Missy away from Ralph, he returned to his own dish beside me. Missy seemed to sense it was safe and returned to her dish next to Ralph. Again, Sam walked over and forcefully separated Missy and Ralph. When it became apparent to us that Sam was not going to allow Ralph to feed Missy, we decided to go home and let the swans settle the matter—what ever the problem was —by themselves. Since late summer, we had noticed another slight change in the birds' relationship. Sam had always been 'Boss Bird' and Missy a willing follower. Now, Missy demanded that she be the leader, with Sam following her lead.

She went so far as to nip at a very surprised Sam, to make her point known. Then for a few days, Sam was the hen-pecked mate. However, when it appeared he could stand it no longer, he nipped at Missy and she became the follower. Swan relationships appeared to be much like their human counterparts; lots of give and take in adjusting to one another.

That year Missy flew away earlier than ever; by the third week in October she migrated. Sam seemed less upset by her departure for there was no frantic search of the harbor. Was it possible that the two swans had a parting of the ways before Missy left? The only way we would know for sure was if she did not return next spring.

Sam and Missy on a moonlit harbor cruise

In the world of swans, Phyllis is Missy's human pet

And Ralph is Sam's human pet.

Chapter Twenty-Two

WINTER RESCUE OF SAM

"Sam sure makes it hard for us to feed him," Ralph lamented when in mid-December an Arctic cold front blasted through and covered all but the center area of the harbor with ice. The swan was sitting on ice twenty yards from shore, south of Island Wharf.

"I'm quite sure Sam was as surprised as we were by the quick formation of ice," I countered.

"He'll have to walk over the ice this time," Ralph said emphatically. "There's no way we can reach him."

When Sam was still stranded on ice three days later, we became anxious about his safety. We knew that swans could go without food for days at a time, but we feared he might become dehydrated without drinking water.

"Something has to be done," Ralph said the next morning as we tried to coax the swan to come to us near the yacht club. "Four days without food should be incentive enough to encourage him to walk over the ice to eat his cornbread."

"We need help, but whom do we call?" I asked.

"I'll see Capt. Bill and Nelson at work today. Maybe they can suggest something," Ralph proposed as we drove home.

"The Fire Department's rescue team is gong to help us get Sam off the ice," Ralph said when he phoned me later that morning.

"Great!" I shouted as relief flowed over me.

"We're to meet at the yacht club at noon. The men will be in their wet suits."

"Aren't the wet suits red?" I asked. "Sam will not like that!" Over the years, we noticed that Sam seemed to dislike the color red. Whenever I wore my red pants, he seemed reluctant come to me.

"Well, Phyllis, we can't tell the rescue team they can't wear red wet suits," Ralph answered, exasperated.

"I know, I know. It's just that Sam will try to escape from them."

"That will probably happen anyway. I'll see you at eleven-thirty."

The rescue team and we arrived at the yacht club at the same time. Four men adorned in fire-engine red wet suits jumped out of the rescue vehicle. Quickly, they decided on a plan of action for the task ahead. A very alert Sam watched what was happening on shore. When the ladders were lowered down over the retaining wall, Sam decided it was time to leave. He tried to get to his feet but the ice was too slick and he could not stand up. As the men walked toward him, his fight or flight mode came into full gear. As he frantically thrashed his wings, he slid farther out on the ice. The ice cracked ominously as the men tried to reach Sam. It was time for a change of plans.

Twenty minutes later, Ralph was at Nye's wharf to meet the rescue team, and climbed aboard the Ram Islander. This thirty-three foot boat ferried the family living on the island in Sippican Harbor from home to town and back. The boat had a steel plate attached to the bow to plow through winter ice. Each mid-December, the Ram Islander brought Santa to town, to the delight of the children gathered at Island Wharf. Now it would help rescue Sam.

Returning to the yacht club, I found a very concerned Sam watching as the boat plowed through the ice. I knew the noise and movement of the boat terrified him but he had to be rescued.

When the boat was within ten feet of the swan, one of the men threw out a lasso, hoping to latch on to him. It fell short and Sam skittered around the bow of the boat. The boat engine rumbled as the captain shoved the gear into reverse and backed off. Another puff of smoke rose from the stack as the boat was put into forward and began to plow through the thicker ice. The move was made quickly, so quickly that Sam did not have a chance to move away. This time the thrown lasso looped around Sam's body and kept him from escaping. As the captain carefully brought the boat up along side the surprised bird, a rescue squad member reached over the side, picked Sam up and put him into the boat.

Photo Courtesy T. Ireland

Before Sam had any time to react to what was happening, Ralph covered him with a blanket. As the boat chugged back to Nye's wharf, I followed in the car.

Triumphantly, Ralph carried the still-covered swan from the boat to our car. I quickly hopped in back to ride with Sam.

"Sam, you're okay," I said as the blanket slid off. A very calm swan sat beside me and looked out the rear window. He showed no signs of panic from all that had happened in the past hour.

"Are you ready to go to your winter home?" a jubilant Ralph asked, the tone of his voice conveyed how relieved he was to have Sam safe. He reached over the seat and stroked the swan's chest. In answer to the 'love-pat,' Sam gently nibbled Ralph's finger.

A few minutes later, we drove into the boatyard. A short walk down the shore and Ralph sat Sam down on the ice. Sam made quick work of reaching the open water and bathed vigorously. He seemed as happy to be at the boatyard as we were to have him there.

A few weeks later, our telephone rang as we finished supper.

Photo Courtesy T. Ireland

"Hi, Mrs. Washburn, I'm Steve from the gym located in Wareham," the man on the telephone said. "I have a problem and maybe you can help. You and your husband take care of a swan, don't you?"

"Yes," I answered. Was Sam in trouble? No, I calmed myself down; we left Sam at the boatyard a few hours ago. There was no way he could be in Wareham.

"I have a swan sleeping in my parking lot," the man continued. "I'm afraid a car driving in the parking lot will hit the bird."

"Is it injured?" I asked.

"I don't think so. It was walking around the parking area for awhile. Now it is sleeping in the middle of the lot."

"We'll be right over," I told him. "Ralph," I called out, hanging up the phone. "We have a rescue mission." I quickly filled him in on the details.

"Grab a sheet," Ralph said as he put on his jacket. "Bring some bread, too."

"What's our plan?" I asked as we drove off.

"If I can get near enough, I'll drop the sheet over it. If it tries to escape, I'll head the swan off and you'll have to drop the sheet over it.

We found the swan all curled up with its head tucked under its wing. Quietly, we got out of the car and approached.

"It must be tired," Ralph commented when the bird did not move as we got nearer. The swan's head popped up as we walked closer. It watched us approach but never stood up as Ralph gently lowered the sheet over the swan. Then he carried the swan to the car and placed it on the back seat, where I joined the bird.

"Are we going to put this swan at the boatyard with Sam?" I asked as we drove off.

"I'm not sure what Sam's reaction would be to another swan appearing out of nowhere in the middle of the night. Let's release it at the Old Landing boat ramp; the water is still open there."

"Bring the bread," Ralph said as he carried the swan down to the water. Once uncovered, the swan walked into the water and began to swim about.

"Throw some bread," Ralph suggested. "Maybe it's hungry."

"It knows bread is good to eat," I said when the swan ate the tossed food.

"It isn't terrified by our presence either," Ralph said.

"Maybe we should have let it go at the boatyard where Sam is," I said, thinking this swan would be an ideal winter companion for Sam.

"No, it is better this way," Ralph reassured me.

When the swan satisfied its hunger, it silently glided off into the darkness. When would the newest arrival discover Sam? What would Sam's reaction be when he first saw the new swan? Would they be friendly toward one another? How long would it be before they met? As always, there were more questions than answers at the beginning of each swan adventure.

The following morning we fed the swans in their separate areas. We decided it was time to give the newest swan a name. "Let's assume the swan is a pen, since the knob over the bill is smaller than Sam's, and name her Lady." Ralph suggested. As far as we knew, it was five days before Lady and Sam met. I cannot tell how the first meeting went for I was not present. But, when we found them together, they were peaceful and there were no battle scars.

As the days of winter passed, we sometimes found Lady at the boatyard with Sam and at other feedings she was at the ice-locked Old Landing shoreline. She used her wings to take her where her wanderlust deemed. Sam took it all in stride. He was not frantic when she flew off, but seemed pleased when she returned.

"Look, Sam's posturing to Lady," Ralph said as we sat in the car after feeding the swans. She answered with a few head nods and went back to bathing.

"Maybe we have a budding romance on our hands," I suggested, as once again Sam postured to Lady and this time she postured back.

For the remainder of the winter the two stayed together, and my hope for cygnets soared once again. In the furthermost reach of my mind, I did think of Missy and wondered what she would do when she found another swan with her Sam. However, it was hard not to be elated over the thought of Lady and Sam becoming a bonded pair.

In spring, as more and more boats entered the harbor, Lady showed signs of uneasiness. One afternoon as we watched the birds from the Old Landing, Sam was heading out of the basin with Lady following close behind.

"She's stopped," Ralph said. "She seems concerned about the approaching boat coming up channel."

"Sam thinks she is still following him," I replied as Sam continued to swim further out of the basin.

"He's just discovered she has stopped," Ralph said. "He's waiting for her to catch up."

"She's refusing to come any farther out into the harbor."

"He's going back for her," Ralph said as Sam turned. When he reached Lady, he nodded, then turned and headed for the open harbor again.

"She's adamant. She not following him," I said as Lady stayed where she was.

A minute later, Sam looked back and saw she was not following him. He turned around and once more swam back to her. This time, the two swans swam back into the quiet basin waters. Lady appeared pleased, while Sam seemed exasperated. She had quietly won.

Although Lady often flew off, leaving Sam alone, she always returned later in the day. Then one day she flew away and never did come back. Sam's reaction was very unconcerned. I wondered, did he expect Missy to come back and was that the reason for the casual relationship he shared with Lady?

Sadly, that was the year even Missy deserted Sam. On her winter sojourn, she must have found an eligible young cob that chased all thoughts of Sam away.

Sam's behavior that late spring seemed to suggest he had had enough with fickle pens. He settled into his bachelor ways once again.

Whenever we spent a night on our moored boat, Sam was an early morning visitor to the Cygnus Olor. One morning I got up extra early to watch the sunrise. There in the mist hanging just over the water surface, a familiar figure glided silently. A few minutes later, a gentle tap-tap on the hull announced his arrival for breakfast.

For the next year and a half, we became a threesome. The special joy we experienced with Sam knew no bounds—until another change occurred.

Chapter Twenty-Three

THE RETURN

"You have to see this," Ralph said when he returned from Sam's morning feeding on the day after Christmas in December 1991. "Get dressed and bundle up."

"What is it?" I asked not wanting to go out in the freezing December air with my nasty cold. "You can tell me."

"I want you to see this. The car is warmed, just come," Ralph urged.

Arriving at the Old Landing, I saw Sam had another swan with him. Now I knew the reason for Ralph's jubilant mood.

"The swan must have arrived early this morning," Ralph continued. "Sam was all alone last night. This swan has known people, for it didn't hesitate to came to eat with Sam."

"Santa must have stopped on his way back to the North Pole," I joked. "He couldn't have chosen a better present for our swan."

"Look at its feet," Ralph exclaimed when Sam's new friend came out of the water at one feeding. "They are a grayish white. This is a Polish mute swan. Do you suppose this swan is Little One all grown up?"

"No, it has been five years since Little One was here as a cygnet. Why would she return now? By this time Little One is old enough to have a mate," I reasoned. "This is just another winter visitor."

"But you've got to admit it could be Little One," Ralph insisted.

Back home, Ralph searched the photo albums for pictures of Little One as I prepared supper.

"Come see this," Ralph called out. "Tell me I'm wrong."

Ralph pointed to a picture of Little One standing on the beach in February of 1986. Looking at the photo, I had to admit the pictured swan looked like a younger version of the swan now with Sam.

"This swan stands pigeon-toed, just like the one in the picture I showed you last night," Ralph said at the next feeding. "That would explain why it is so trusting."

Just then the bird stretched, and flapped her wings. She appeared to stand on tiptoes as her powerful wings almost lifted her off the ground. The force of her flexing wings sent dead leaves and sand eddying about the beach.

"Look! Look"! Ralph said excitedly. "There's an inverted feather like the one we saw in Little One's photo last night. It's even in the same spot as the one in the photo. That's the clincher; this swan is Little One!"

We had already tried to pick a name for the newest arrival. However, we couldn't agree on one. No name was needed; Little One had returned.

Memories of a young Little One flooded my mind. I recalled a cygnet that raised her wings to make herself look big and bad as she hissed loudly to frighten me away as she approached the feeding dish. Then came the questions: Why had Little One returned? Why was she alone? Had her mate jilted her? Had her mate died flying into power lines?

"Sam appears elated with Little One's return," I remarked one afternoon as we watched our birds return to the water after feeding. "Do you think Sam knows it is Little One or does he just feel that another swan has flown in for a winter visit?"

"We'll never know the answer to that question. Look, they are blowing bubbles and posturing with one another like they're beginning to bond. Maybe they will mate this spring."

The Daggett House brook became the swans' winter home when a super cold spell arrived. Feeding the birds at times of high tides was easy because the swans could swim to us. However, low tides presented a challenge, as the brook became a small trickle surrounded by mud flats and ice floes. The swans pushed themselves through the small rivulet of the water on their bellies until there was no water to help them slide over the mud. Then they got to their feet and walked the rest of the way. Black mud spattered everything in range. When Sam seemed reluctant to push himself upstream at low tide, we went to him, using the rocks in the brook for stepping-stones.

As winter turned to spring, the swans began to court more and more. With the run of the harbor, they chose to spend most of their days in Hammett Cove, but returned to the Old Landing for their meals.

"Now where are they?" Ralph asked when we arrived at the usual feeding spot and the swans were not there.

"Maybe they are on their way."

"Let's go to Tabor," Ralph suggested after a half-hour of waiting. "We can see if they are coming."

"The next spot to check is the campground beach," Ralph said when we did not locate the swans. However, they were not there either so we continued our search. It was in a quiet marsh inlet in Jenney Cove that we found our birds. From that time on, the swans chose that marsh for their new home. Here we were alone with them, except for an occasional visitor.

"Do you think they have returned to the Old Landing?" I asked one afternoon when we arrived to find no swans waiting at the marsh.

*The roughness and lines on Sam's bill testifies to the
many lifetime battles he has survived*

"We are early. We'll wait awhile; they may be swimming in from Hammett Cove."

Ralph turned on the car radio and I picked up the book I usually carried with me when going to feed the swans. I enjoyed reading while we waited for our friends.

"Sam's coming," Ralph announced, as the bird appeared, swimming out from behind some marsh brush with Little One following so closely she was almost touching his tail. "Do you suppose they are searching out a nest site up that tidal ditch?"

"That would be a secluded spot for a nest. But how safe?" I wondered.

"When the tide is out they would be stranded there. We know there are raccoons and foxes around here."

"Another reason to worry," I said.

"I'll let you finish feeding them," Ralph said a little later, "I want to check out the tidal ditch and see where it leads."

After eating, the birds sat on the marsh and preened before they returned to the water. Once in, they began their courting ritual. With necks straight, they approached one another and head postured, looking first to the left and then to the right. They spoke to one another in soft, short grunts. A few minutes later, Sam's wings began to rise and I looked up to see Ralph walking across the marsh.

"That's one secluded spot," he reported. "Its located at the end of the ditch, there is a large crop of marsh reed. The swans are beginning to clear a spot for a nest."

"How far in is it?" I asked.

"About 200-300 feet. They've already cleared an area of about five feet in diameter. They had to be working most of the afternoon on it. They can only get there at high tide. Half-way up there's a bush growing in the ditch. They have to crawl up the bank to get by it."

I remembered reading that swans usually nest near water, sometimes out on the open marsh. Why had our swans chosen such a secluded site? The swans did not return to nest building for a few days. Then one day when the birds were not waiting for us, Ralph again walked to the nest site.

"They are building," he reported upon his return. "Both are cutting down the reeds and laying them in a circular pile."

"Did they see you?"

"I don't think so; I tried to be as quiet as possible. A branch cracked under my foot but they continued cutting the reed."

We waited for the swans to come to eat. When they did arrive, both were covered with black mud because the tide was going out. When we left them, they were strenuously bathing to remove the grime off their white feathers.

"Let's walk to the nest site," Ralph suggested when a week later we did not find the swans waiting. "They must be working on the nest."

"Should we disturb them? I don't want to frighten them off. Maybe Little One is close to laying her eggs."

"We'll approach from the field on the other side of the ditch."

"Here, grab my hand," Ralph whispered when I tried to hop across the ditch. The ground on the other side was a carpet of bright green moss so my landing was soft and silent. A couple of yards further on gave us a view through the tall reeds of two swans at work.

"That's Sam sitting in the center," a surprised Ralph said.

"I thought it was the pen's duty to build the nest."

"Maybe they take turns cutting the reeds down and constructing it."

We watched, fascinated, as Little One gnawed at the base of the reed, making it sway back and forth before the reed finally fell to the ground. Next she picked the reed up in her bill and passed it over to her mate. Sam picked up the reed. Sometimes he broke it into smaller pieces before placing it on the nest site. We watched as Sam slowly worked at building up the sides of the nest. Every so often he stood up and turned around to work on another section. We observed the birds for quite awhile and then left before they saw or sensed our presence, not wanting to discourage the nesting instinct.

Most days the swans spent hours building the nest. Then a few weeks later, as if a switch was turned off, they abandoned the project and settled into a carefree life style. This sudden halt to nest building puzzled us at first. Then we read in a swan article that a mated pair of mute swans usually does not produce cygnets that first year. They go through all the motions of mating and nest building, but it is in the second year that cygnets are born.

The summer passed with enjoyable hours spent feeding and playing with our swans. With the arrival of late fall, Sam and Little One settled in at the Old Landing for the winter. When the harbor iced over, the swans were down near the Tabor dock.

"This is going to be a problem," Ralph said when we arrived one morning to find Tabor's docking float ice-bound. The swans were hemmed in near the boulders where another under-ground rivulet emptied into the harbor and kept the water open. We trudged through the eight inches of freshly fallen snow. When we reached the birds, we discovered snow and ice covered the slanting retaining wall.

"We'll have to throw the food to them this morning," I said.

"This isn't working," Ralph said when the circling gulls grabbed the food before the swans could reach it. "I'll try crawling down the breakwater to reach them, then you can slide the bread and cornbread down to me."

Cautiously Ralph inched himself down the slippery stones. The swans ate the food with a contentment fit for a king.

"Careful," Ralph warned as I started to throw loose snow at the circling hungry gulls. "If you lose your balance, you'll slide down the embankment and go right through the ice."

"I'm being careful," I answered, intent on chasing the pesky birds away. They could fly to open water to eat. Sam did not have that option.

Lots of snow fell that year, so we were pleased the swans chose Tabor's waterfront as their winter home. Tabor Academy kept the parking lot plowed so we could reach the swans daily. By the end of February, humans and swans were anxiously waiting for spring to arrive.

Little One's unique eye color and pale feet, different from the other swans we have observed, is a trait of the Polish swan.

Chapter Twenty-Four

THE BONDING

As soon as the cove was free of ice, Sam and Little One returned to last year's summer home and never returned to the Old Landing. We saw signs of the swans mating as March turned to April but there was no nest construction. Through research, I learned that mute swans mate in early spring and the cygnets hatch in late April after a thirty to thirty-five day incubation period.

"Are you watching?" Ralph asked one day as we stayed to observe the swans after feeding them. The swans were swimming and bathing in Briggs' Cove, their new home base. Side by side, they bathed in unison. Next they began to head posture and soon were dipping their heads in the water and blowing bubbles. They communicated to one another in short soft grunts and purrs while posturing continued. Then the head dipping became emphatic and water splashed everywhere.

They came together, gave a sharp loud grunt, and raised their heads in unison skyward. Breast rubbing, head posturing, and the alternating placing of their necks over the other's back followed this. The mating tempo built. Finally, Sam mounted Little One from the back; he held the back of her neck with his bill, almost forcing her head underwater. A minute or two later Sam slipped off her back. The swans made strong dips in the water, almost submerging their bodies. Subsequently, they stretched their heads straight up and each gave a trumpet call. Next there followed, an entwining of their necks as both thrashed their feet to gain further height. With the mating-bond completed, each began to preen their feathers.

"Wow, wasn't that something!" Ralph broke the silence. "Not too many people get to witness that."

"That's for sure," I answered, while knowing I felt like an interloper at having witnessed the mating.

"They haven't started nest construction yet," Ralph commented. "I wonder how long a time there is between mating and the laying of eggs."

"Maybe fertilization of the egg does not always happen on the first try, like in humans."

Although we both thought there would be a flurry of nest building activity, it was not until a week later that the swans began building a nest. April's full moon arrived with a higher than normal high tide and the nest site flooded. The next day Sam and Little One began to build a new nest, in sight of the first one but on higher ground. That day's moon-tide proved that the second nest would be out of danger of being flooded, except for a coastal storm's tidal surge.

"Let's walk by the swans' nest site to see how the construction is coming," Ralph suggested a few days later.

"We shouldn't disturb them," I answered. Their nest was so close to the sidewalk—right out in the open.

"We won't let them see us," Ralph countered. "We'll just walk by without stopping to look. The swans will think we are strangers walking by."

"Little One is building the nest, Sam's gathering the reeds," Ralph whispered as we passed the swans' nest site. I had kept my eyes straight ahead.

On our return trip by the nest site, we stopped behind a tall cedar and watched the construction activity. Sam gnawed at the base of a tall reed, and then he picked it up with his bill and passed it over to Little One. She placed it on the nest. If she had a design plan in her mind, it was not evident to us as she placed each reed in a different spot, never side by side in a methodical scheme.

"Let's go," I urged, not wanting to disturb the nesting instinct. However, the swans were so intent on nest building that our movement on the sidewalk did not pique their attention.

"No eggs yet," Ralph announced a couple days later when the two

swans came swimming out of the marsh inlet that led to their nest site.

"Patience, patience, neither of us has any idea how long it takes a pen to develop a fertilized egg. We do know there can be four to six eggs in the nest but don't know how long it takes her to lay the eggs."

A few days later, on a mid-day visit, we did not find the swans in sight. As we passed their nest site, we were surprised to see Little One

sitting in the center of the second nest while Sam was busy constructing yet another nest. Encouraged and hoping that Little One was finally laying her eggs, we left quickly.

Our euphoria was dashed when both swans were waiting to be fed that night.

"I'm going to check the nest," Ralph said. "Maybe there's an egg in it. Keep their attention on eating."

Sam, always in charge of what Sam does, ignored my demands for him to stay with me when he saw Ralph walking along the sidewalk near the nest site. He entered the water, swam slowly toward the nest with his wings raised. Little One followed Sam. A few minutes later, when Ralph started to come back, both birds stopped swimming to the nest and began to head dip and blow bubbles. Soon they were posturing with one another. However, this time there was no mating. Before long, each was searching under water for food.

Over the course of a month's time, we found the swans in the nest site several times. One day they spent the whole day there, Little One sitting in the nest with Sam close by. Was she about to start laying eggs? Or was she sitting in the middle of the large nest for inspiration?

To our great disappointment, Little One never did lay an egg. The veterinarian had warned us not to become optimistic when we told him the swans were nest building and mating. Sam was an old bird, he stressed, maybe too old. Later, when we reported to him that Little One never did lay an egg, he explained that was a sign that she was sterile. Even if Sam could not fertilize her, Little One would still lay the eggs.

By late May, the swans abandoned the nest as the mating urge passed. Life for them settled into a routine of eating, swimming, and sun bathing on the banking. All seemed right with the world until one stormy day when the birds did not appear for breakfast.

"I'm going to walk the shore line of the cove," a very concerned Ralph announced when the swans did not appear by noon. "Sam hasn't been acting like himself lately. Maybe he's hurt and can't come to us."

"I'll wait here just in case they come. One of us should be here."

An hour and a half later, a very worried Ralph returned to report he did not find the swans. That was very much out of the ordinary.

"I checked each marsh ditch between here and the mouth of the cove. Sam could have swum up a ditch and became stranded when the tide went out."

"Let's check the harbor area; maybe they returned to the basin and are waiting for us to show up there to feed them."

Our search was fruitless. Our concerns grew as the hours passed without the swans' return. Not until the next morning did we see our swans. Both were waiting for breakfast in the cove when we arrived. Sam was a very bedraggled and dirty looking bird. His white feathers had a reddish-brown hue to them, with smudges of black mud.

"Something's wrong," Ralph declared as we watched the swan try to walk up the slight incline to his dish. "Sam can't get himself up on shore." Ralph was out of the car and half way down to the swan before he finished the sentence.

As Sam tried to gain footing on the grass, Ralph reached down and picked him up. When he placed Sam down on the grass, the swan collapsed and fell to the ground; he could not stand.

"What's happened, Sam?" Ralph questioned the swan. "Look at his legs when I lift him up," he instructed me. "Maybe one is broken."

"I don't see any signs of injury. Set him down gently. Maybe the leg was stiff and now it will support his weight."

"His left leg seems to be the problem," Ralph answered as he set him down again. Once again Sam collapsed on the ground, leaning to the left. Ralph put his hand under the pad of the foot and pushed against it, to see if Sam had any strength in that leg to push back. There appeared to be some strength but not enough to hold Sam upright.

While the swans ate, we pondered what we could do for Sam. Other than not being able to stand, Sam appeared normal, eating as usual.

"Let's stop to see Dr. Tremblay on our way home. Maybe he can tell us what's wrong with Sam." The vet suggested we bring Sam in for a visit. He wanted to x-ray the left leg to confirm the problem was arthritis and not an injury.

The next day at breakfast we captured Sam. We left what seemed to be a very confused Little One alone. Little One's expression at seeing us drive off with her Sam seemed to show alarm, bewilderment, and worry. Our emotions at that moment were mixed: great concern for Sam's health and deep sadness at separating the two swans. It was to be a short separation, for the vet's office was just up the street from the cove.

At the Marion Animal Hospital, Ralph gently placed Sam on the x-ray table and tried to keep him from rolling off it. Sam did not approve of what was happening when the vet turned him on his back. After the vet took the x-ray, Ralph quickly up-righted Sam and gave him some comforting stroking.

Dr. Tremblay returned with the x-ray that showed a flurry of white around his knee-joint. (On a swan this is located way up on the leg, hidden by body feathers). He said that Sam probably injured his arthritic knee-joint and that was the reason he was unable to stand on the left leg. He gave us some tetracycline to clear up any infection. He did not suggest a complete cure, but thought Sam would regain use of that leg.

For awhile, Sam seemed to get better. Maybe it was our hoping to have him back to his old self that made us think we saw improvement in his condition. Never a graceful walker on land, Sam hobbled worse than ever, but he did manage to move about.

Two weeks later Ralph went alone to give the swans their evening meal. When he did not find them waiting for their meal, he checked to see if the swans were around the nest site. Although the mating instinct had ended, the swans often returned to that spot to rest.

A heart wrenching sight greeted him there. He found Sam lying on his back in the marsh ditch. First Sam thrashed his right leg in the air trying to get upright. Then he tried to use the left leg without success. Ralph ran to Sam and quickly picked him up. With an incoming tide, if Ralph had not found him, Sam would have drowned. After placing Sam on higher ground and giving him some food, Ralph rushed home to telephone me at the meeting I was attending.

"Sam's in trouble again," he said, his voice filled with worry. "Come quick. Is there someone who can give you a ride to the cove? I want to get back to Sam. He's so covered with black mud he looks more like a black swan than a white mute swan. I want to clean the mud off him."

"I'll get a ride," I answered as Ralph stopped to catch his breath. "Take some fresh water from home back with you. What do you think happened?"

"I'll use sea water. Sam probably tried to climb out of the ditch, lost his balance and tumbled over on his back and couldn't upright himself. Hurry."

When I arrived, Ralph was attempting to wipe the black mud off our friend, without much luck.

"Let's take him home," Ralph said. "We can hose him down to get him clean. We'll use a gentle spray."

"But we don't have anything to sit him on," I pointed out. "There will be mud all over the back seat."

"Use the towels I brought from home, I grabbed an armful."

Since darkness had fallen, we placed Sam in the glare of our back yard spotlight to clean him. He was docile, but barked out his displeasure at our using the hose to clean him. However, he must have sensed we were trying to help, for he sat still. After toweling him as dry as possible we packed him in the car and took him back to the cove and Little One, who was still sitting where we left her. Ralph placed Sam beside his mate. Although night had fallen, we stayed with the swans, talking softly to them. Finally, with heavy hearts, we left wondering what we would find in the morning.

To our relief, the swans were in the water waiting for our arrival. When Sam still could not climb up on the bank, Ralph picked him up and placed him in front of his dish. He was so hungry he ate the cornbread two or three pieces at a time. Other than Sam's usually white feathers looking slightly grungy, there was no outward sign he was experiencing any difficulty. We noted he was no longer as meticulously clean; a trace of marsh mud etched some of the feathers.

"Sam's lower body feathers look water-logged," Ralph observed. "It must be that he can't reach over his back to the oil gland at the base of his tail."

"I can't recall the last time I saw him preen and oil his feathers," I answered. "There's a faint water line mark on his lower body."

"As he loses the oil protection off the feathers, he sits lower in the water."

"Should we try to rub him down with baby oil?" I asked.

"I wouldn't, there may be a chemical in it that could harm him," Ralph replied. "We'll watch him closely for a few days. The water is warm so there's no danger of his dying from hypothermia. I think Sam still has enough oil on his body to keep him from sinking."

On a stormy day a few weeks later, the swans were once again missing. Ralph checked and rechecked the cove throughout the day. Then in the late afternoon, he found Sam, alone, trying to climb up on the bank. Ralph's heart almost broke watching a rain-soaked, grungy-looking Sam valiantly trying to gain a foothold on the shore. It was too much for Ralph. He picked up his beloved friend and brought him home.

Chapter Twenty-Five

SAM, SAM

"Phyl, Phyl, I need help out here," Ralph shouted as he rang the doorbell frantically. "I brought Sam home. He's a mess; bring out some towels so I can wipe him down."

One look at the bedraggled Sam, dirty and drenched from the day's downpours, sent my heart into a tailspin. He no longer looked like the majestic white swan that swam to us looking for his meal the past eleven years. Ralph's face was etched with worry.

"It's going to take more than towel drying to clean off this mud," Ralph said. "Turn on the hose."

Sam was calm as we washed and fed him. Was this another instance that he sensed we wanted to help him?

"Where are we going to put him tonight?"

"Let's put him in the shed," Ralph suggested.

"But what will we do with him while we empty it?" I asked. Sam was calm now but there was no guarantee he would remain so.

"We'll make a small fence around him with the left-over wire garden fencing."

"He'll push it over unless we stake it."

"He's not going to go anywhere; he can hardly move. It will take longer to stake the fence than to quickly clean out the shed."

A half-hour later, Sam was housed in the shed and eating cornbread.

Later I drove to the cove to give Little One her supper, but she was not there. Had Little One deserted her Sam? Had she flown off with another cob? That did not seem possible to me. Sadly, I went back home.

The next morning when we opened the shed door to feed Sam I thought he seemed to have a resigned look about him, but he heartily ate breakfast. I wondered what kind of a night he had. Had he experienced fear at being in a strange place or did he feel safe sleeping in a building? Sam had not moved during the night; could he have moved if he wanted to? Those questions went unanswered.

"He's calling for Little One," Ralph said when Sam trumpeted the 'where are you' call we heard him use when Missy disappeared. "Little One is probably searching for him in the cove."

"Why don't you go feed her while I construct a penned yard for Sam? We'll keep him here for a few days, at least until he can move about."

I found Little One searching for Sam. She readily came to eat, but once finished she began looking for her missing mate. She even swam up the marsh ditch that led to the nest site and then headed out of the cove. My heart ached for her and Sam, the separated lovers.

Back home, I discovered Ralph had completed the small-penned area and a very docile Sam was sitting in the middle of it. Every so often, he gave that mournful trumpet call.

After a morning of hearing Sam's calls for his missing mate, we decided to take him down to the shore to visit Little One. It was only to be a visit for we knew that Sam, not being able to move about, would be in dire danger if we left him on the shore. At least they would be together for a little while, which we reasoned was better than being totally separated.

"Call Little One," Ralph instructed when we saw her swimming off the campground beach. "I'll bring Sam to the area near the overturned skiffs. It will be hard for him to move around them to reach the water, in case he tries to go for a swim. If he gets in the water, we'll lose control."

"Little One," I called, holding up my bag of food. To my surprise, she readily came to me. Just then, she saw Ralph put Sam down. Her steps quickened as she almost ran up the shore toward Sam. He was valiantly trying to push his body over the ground to reach her.

As they got closer to each other, the swans exchanged numerous head nods. They greeted each other with short purr-voice conversations. I wished I knew what they were saying to one another. With all the head nodding and soft vocal exchanges between them, I decided it had to be 'happy talk.'

When Little One sat down next to Sam, Ralph brought the feeding dishes from the car and the birds ate a 'breakfast for two.' Finishing their meal, the swans sat quietly, appearing to be content just being together.

"Woof, woof," a black dog barked as he came around a near-by house. Another dog appeared, and then a third dog followed. Getting to her feet, Little One gave a loud hiss, raising her wings ever higher and outward, and then she gave a louder hiss. The dogs stopped, heeded her warning, and left the swans alone.

"The birds aren't safe here," Ralph said. "Little One could handle one dog at a time but not three. While she was fighting-off one dog, the other two could harm Sam. Let's take Sam back home and bring Little One too."

"We can't carry Little One and Sam at the same time in the car," I reminded him.

"I know that. I'll go home to get Peter and the truck. You stay here with the birds."

"Just hurry," I urged. I was glad our son Peter, a pilot with a Providence layover, was here to help us.

In what seemed a long time to me, but was actually a fifteen— twenty minute time span, Ralph returned in the car with Peter following in the truck. In the bed of the truck rested the huge carton that we had used to rescue a stranded Sam off the ice at Black Point.

Little One became concerned as Peter backed the truck up twenty feet from where we were sitting. I was afraid she would decide to retreat to the water and thwart our plan.

"We'll pick up Little One first," Ralph said in a matter of fact voice. With his engineer-brain in charge, he already knew how to accomplish this task.

"What do you want me to do?" I asked.

"Just keep Sam content, prevent him from moving toward the water if he should become alarmed when I pick Little One up."

That I could do. My only concern was that I might hurt Sam if I restrained him.

Before I had time for more thought, Ralph had Little One pinned to the ground and Peter was bringing over the box. I thought Sam's face had a worried look but he did not attempt to move.

"So far so good," Ralph commented as he slipped Little One inside the carton, quickly folded the top flaps over her, and secured the box with clothesline rope. Quickly, he and Peter carried the boxed swan to the truck.

A few minutes later, Sam and I were settled in the back seat of the car. On the short trip home, Ralph followed the truck with Little One riding in the body. I feared that Little One would panic, try to escape, and end up falling out of the truck, box and all.

"The penned yard is too small for two swans," Ralph said as he put the swans inside it. "I'll make it larger after lunch."

"And what will we do with them while you do that?" I asked.

"I'll just build the larger yard around the small one. They can stay in the smaller one and watch me work."

Suddenly the enormity of what was ahead of us sank in. Would the shed be big enough to hold both swans during the night? Would they get in each other's way and become cantankerous? Had we made the right choice by bringing Little One home too? Would she be content to be with Sam and not miss swimming in the cove? At the moment, both birds appeared satisfied with the choices we had made for them.

"Sam seems happy to have his sweetie with him," Ralph said at the end of the afternoon as he removed the smaller fence to give the swans the larger fenced-in yard.

"I'm just happy to have them together." I almost sang from the pure joy of it.

Little One seemed delighted to be with Sam! She did not seem to mind being away from the cove. All the while, we kept a watchful eye on the swans, ever fearful that a dog would wander through the yard and discover the birds.

"It's time to put the birds in the shed," Ralph said as dusk fell.

"Who's going in first?" I asked.

"Sam," he answered. "You'll have to watch Little One in case she tries to follow him."

Little One, ever attentive, watched as Ralph picked up Sam. When they disappeared from her sight, Little One gave a loud 'where-are-you' trumpet call. She gave another trumpet call when Ralph picked her up. Little One's neck stretched straight forward and her feet fanned the air as Ralph carried her to Sam. She seemed to be one happy swan when he placed her in the shed with Sam.

"That went smoothly," Ralph said. "This is another first for Little One tonight. I wonder what she'll think about sleeping inside the shed."

"I think both of them will be more content being together again," I said.

Two swans were eating from the same dish as we closed the door.

In the morning, we found them sitting side by side, facing a dish completely emptied of grass and corn. After giving them breakfast, Ralph carried the swans to their yard.

"We have to figure a way to let the birds bathe," Ralph noted another problem. "My guess is that they will be house guests for several days."

"Let's get the old inflatable wading pool we used years ago for our children out of the cellar," I suggested. "The old latex may still hold air." This was not the reason I had been holding on to it for so long. Never in my wildest dreams would I have thought about using it as a bathing pool for a pair of swans.

After huffing and puffing to blow the sides up and filling it with water, Ralph gently placed Sam in it. First thing he did was take a drink and then another and another. Little One watched from the sideline but did not attempt to enter the pool. When Ralph picked her up and placed her beside Sam in the pool, she immediately stepped out of it. Obviously, she did not think it was a suitable substitute for the cove.

Realizing that one of the swans' claws could puncture the plastic, we decided to buy a rigid plastic pool, the largest we could find. The larger pool was a better fit; Sam appeared to enjoy sitting in the water. Little One looked funny standing full height in a child's wading pool with the water coming only half way up her legs. However, it gave us a sense of helping the swans live in our backyard.

Sam sat and appeared to enjoy being in the water

Ralph even tried giving Sam physical therapy

As Sam aged he often enjoyed sitting on the shore visiting with us, basking in the sun

At that time we still hoped to return the birds to the cove when Sam improved and could move about on his own. Ralph even tried giving Sam physical therapy. He placed Sam on a low stool with a couch pillow as a cushion and let him move his left foot back and forth in the air. Sam was trying to get off the stool but the bad left leg did not make contact with the ground. Sometimes Ralph would push against the left pad hoping to bring back strength to that weak foot. Little One watched silently from a distance.

As the days and weeks passed, we came to realize that we might have the birds with us longer than we first thought. The 5' x 6' shed and the garden wire fenced yard were inadequate and unsafe as a semi-permanent home. Returning from a visit to the local building supply store, our truck carried a 10' x 10' shed kit and five 6' x 6' kennel fencing frames. A few days later we went back to the store and bought two windows for the shed, as I felt the birds would be happier if they had a view of the yard from inside their 'birdhouse.'

Early the next morning, our grandson David came to help dig out where we wanted to place the shed. We chose a spot under two large shade trees so the shed wouldn't get too hot from the summer sun beating down on it. It was hard digging, for there were roots from an old lilac bush that had been spreading for years. David and Ralph spent the day moving dirt, chopping roots and prying a couple of large stones out of the way. Sam and Little One watched the progress from their penned yard.

After a full week of intensive work, Ralph proudly placed the two birds inside their new home for the first time. The next morning, Ralph set the kennel fence in place, making a penned yard in front of the door. We breathed easier knowing that our swans were safer than they had ever been. We named the swans' new home 'Sam's Place' in honor of its special resident.

However, that was not the end of construction. Before long we covered the shed floor with linoleum, and Ralph built a dirt ramp covered with artificial grass to make it easier for the birds to access the building.

Sam still could not use the left leg to climb and the small step up impeded his moving in and out of the building. Then we bought more

kennel panels to enlarge their penned yard to a 24' x 24' dimension. The next project was to place the wading pool in ground and add a small fountain to give Sam the option of a shower instead of the bathing that appeared difficult for him. It was obvious that Sam approved of the addition of the fountain, for he often sat under it for ten to fifteen minutes, just having the water showering over his back.

At first the five-foot wading pool seemed ideal until we watched two swans try to swim in it at the same time; then it was side to side swans. Ralph's solution was to enlarge the pool by bonding another wading pool to the first one.

When fall arrived and we realized the swans would be permanent houseguests, Ralph insulated the shed for winter. When winter settled in, Ralph disconnected the fountain, wrapped the water pipes with heater tapes, and made a movable plywood-insulated cover for the pool. This made it possible for the swans to have bathing privileges during winter. When the temperature dipped into the teens, we purchased a small electrical heater, which Ralph modified to come on at a temperature of 25 degrees and shut off at 36 degrees. Next Ralph, a lover of good music, suggested a stereo system for the swans, but I vetoed the idea. That would really get people saying we had definitely gone overboard in providing the necessities of life for our birds.

The swans had many visitors. For more than twenty years Sam had been Sippican Harbor's unofficial mascot; people missed seeing him and came to visit him. Even the local walking group routed some of their walks around visits to see Sam and Little One. One grandpa regularly brought his granddaughter to see Sam.

Chapter Twenty-Six

THE PARTING

Winter passed with no change in Sam's health. He was able to move about minimally. On warm sunny winter days we opened both doors and let Sam enjoy the meager warmth of the winter sun from inside the building while being out of the reach of the cold north wind.

I think we both knew that Sam's time with us was getting shorter, but neither of us put the thought into words. We made him as comfortable as possible. The pool water was kept warmed to forty degrees so Sam would not be cold when Ralph gently placed our beloved guest in it to clean himself. I think even Little One knew something of what was happening to her Sam, for she stayed close to him. At night, they slept side by side. That was how we found them on the March 1995 morning we discovered Sam's earthly journey had ended. Little One was right beside him. Sam had peacefully placed his head over his back and quietly passed away. Only someone who has loved an animal completely will understand the depth of our sorrow that March morning.

I had a vividly graphic dream the night Sam died - a dream that woke me at 3 a.m. In my dream I was on our boat in the harbor...near one of Sam's favorite spots along the shore...a full moon filled the harbor with soft light...a group of tall dark cedar trees lined the shore...a hazy cloud passed over the moon and in the semi-darkness I saw a beautiful white swan take to the air on two powerful wings and fly away from me.

That morning as I walked down the stairs, a tremendous emptiness filled my heart. Ralph went out alone to check on the swans. His quick return and the tears on his cheeks answered the question I did not need to ask. We held each other tightly, as there were no words to ease the deep sorrow that flooded our beings.

We returned to Sam's Place together to find Little One still sitting close to Sam. We gently wrapped Sam in the old purple jacket that I had worn so many times while feeding him. Silently we did what had to be done. We dug a deep grave in our backyard near where Sam lived his final days. Today a swan planter given by our daughter Debbie marks the spot.

Little One expressed her sorrow with that same beseeching 'where are you' call she used when Sam was out of sight. For a week or two whenever Little One walked out of her house, she called for Sam. We ached for her but there was nothing we could do to ease the sorrow she seemed to be feeling.

Neither a cygnet-size stuffed swan nor a trio of floating yellow rubber ducks eased her loneliness. Five weeks later when we found no injured swan needing a home, we did the next best thing for our

grieving swan. We adopted a duck that we named Max. The man who owned Max was anxious to give him to us as a fox had just killed his Canada goose. Max had followed the Canada goose around like a shadow. It took awhile, but Little One and Max became feathered friends.

One summer's day a year and a half after Sam died, Ralph and I were aboard our boat, the Cygnus Olor, reading and relaxing. The sound of swan wings in flight brought us both to our feet. We searched the sky hoping to see a swan in flight. However, neither of us saw a swan soaring off in the distance. Was it Sam's spirit passing overhead to let us know he was once again flying high?

SAM CIRCA 1963 – 1995

Epilogue

Little One lived another fourteen years after Sam died. On a cold January day in 2009 Little One died from what appeared to be a stroke at the age of twenty-four years. In her final years she lived alone with only us as companions. Loving memories now bring comfort to our grieving hearts as we live life without swan friends.

Our twenty-four years of life among mute swans has enriched our lives with a full measure of joy. The opportunity to know Sam, Missy, Little One and other swans in such intimate relationships has increased our love, awe and knowledge of these magnificent birds.